This
Is It.

'Conor is Ireland's answer to Sam Harris. This book will teach you truly life-altering wisdom that has stood the test of both time and science in the most hilarious, relatable and heart-warmingly, welcoming way.'

DANIELLA MOYLES

'I love Conor's way of sharing the magic of contemplation and meditation. In a world filled with distraction and noise, Conor reminds us to slow down and come back to ourselves.'

PAT DIVILLY

'Other-worldly and painfully, beautifully Irish all at once. Like poetry and philosophy read by your brother's best friend who has been around the world and come back to serve you everything you've forgotten you already know. I adore this book and Conor.'

ANGELA SCANLON

This Is It.

Conor Creighton

Gill Books

Gill Books
Hume Avenue
Park West
Dublin 12
www.gillbooks.ie

Gill Books is an imprint of M.H. Gill and Co.

Designed by iota (www.iota-books.ie)
Copy-edited by Jane Rogers
Proofread by Neil Burkey
Printed by ScandBook in Sweden

This book is typeset in Apolline.
The paper used in this book comes
from the wood pulp of managed
forests. For every tree felled, at least
one tree is planted, thereby renewing
natural resources.

This book is dedicated to my mum and dad.
I wouldn't be here without them.

Contents

Introduction

I wrote this book during the first stage of the Covid-19 lockdown in an apartment in the Neukölln area of Berlin. It was a time of seeming impossibilities. I grew tomatoes on a cold, north-facing window; I strengthened my friendships, although I only saw friends on Zoom; and I fell apart and put myself back together again, all from the comfort of my kitchen.

I'd been living in Berlin for over ten years but had just made the decision to move back to Ireland and become a full-time meditation teacher. I'd returned to Berlin to finish a meditation course I'd begun with a group of Syrian refugees, only for the pandemic to hit. I was landed with a decision: do I stay in Berlin and just put my plans aside, or do I go home to my parents and risk infecting them? My father was high-risk. When I talk to my friends I recognise that most of our fathers are high-risk. Medically and emotionally.

In the end I stayed in Berlin, and those plans – a new series of courses in Dublin, a retreat at the Cliffs of Moher and a number of studios who all wanted me to teach regular slots – fell through. I couldn't complain. None of us really could. 'The rain falls equally on all things' is one of my favourite Zen expressions, and at the time it felt that this was true. Everything was unprecedented. Nobody felt in control. We were all, to different degrees, sinking more than swimming. Here's something good I heard once: admitting that you're not in control of what's around you is the first step to establishing control inside you.

I never imagined that I would teach meditation. I certainly never imagined that I'd write a book about it. I sincerely hope I've done a good job.

I taught some of my first workshops in the artist Maser's studio in Dublin. Huge pipes criss-crossed the ceiling carrying water from the flats above. They sounded like rain sticks, the kind you might hear at a soundbath or early morning at a house party in east Clare played by the one guy who didn't take mushrooms, he's just like that all the time.

At the end of one of those classes a woman came up to me and pointed at the simple Tibetan bowl that I used to signal the beginning and end of each meditation.

'Are you sure that's such a good idea?'

'Why?'

'It's triggering,' she said.

'It is?' I asked.

'It sounds like a mass bell. Every time you bang it, I get the shivers.'

'Do you think I should ditch it?'

'I would, yeah,' she said.

I never brought the metal bowl to class again, and swapped it for a solid oak one that could only have triggered someone who'd been traumatised by woodpeckers.

I've always found teaching meditation in Ireland a unique experience compared to everywhere else I worked. If I ever used the Irish weather as a way of explaining the concept of change, people got me in a way that my students in Los Angeles, where it rains all of three days every year, didn't. Or if I talked about death, and the importance of integrating it into our daily life, I knew that most of my class had probably seen a body in an open casket at a traditional Irish funeral, but none of my other European students would have. And if I wanted to talk about the unique capacity of nature to momentarily tame the mind, and bring you to places and states reminiscent of deep meditative practice, it wasn't hard for people to imagine that unique power, because in Ireland you're never far from some mist-bejewelled, rainbow-bordered, geographic manifestation of what might just be god.

There's a cryptic old expression that the veil is thin in Ireland, meaning that the boundary between the rational and the spiritual worlds are not as thick in Ireland as they are in other places. I don't know if this is true. Meditation, to begin with, is not magic, it's actually highly scientific, but to believe in it, to actually see it work, you have to have some patience, an open mind and not a little bit of hope. Hope is hardwired into Irish people. I grew up following a national football team who taught me so much about the thrill of crushing defeat that I feel uncomfortable with victory. The hope creeps into our choices. I set off hiking on many a sunny morning that transformed into a winter squall by lunchtime, and I knew so many young men who died young – in road accidents, by suicide and sudden deaths – that it felt like there was a certain amount of luck, and maybe hope, involved in surviving your twenties in rural Ireland.

There are many things hardwired into us Irish people. My intention in writing this book was to explore the ways that meditation, and contemplation, and the simple folk wisdom you learn from just watching time pass, are actually hardwired into us too.

This book is a meditation guide. It will show you the benefits of meditation and the special Irish connection to meditation, but, most important, it will show you how to meditate.

There was a great Indian meditation teacher called Jiddu Krishnamurti. He moved to California and hung out with Aldous Huxley and Allen Ginsberg and Timothy Leary, and a whole host of other acid hippy-intellectuals. Aldous Huxley's niece was my landlady and neighbour when I lived in California, and she'd come down every morning and shout Krishnamurti's quotes through the window of the metal storage container I was renting from her. This was my favourite: 'There is great happiness in not wanting, in not being something, in not going somewhere.'

Long before him, in some field in Connemara, an unknown Irish farmer, probably struggling to keep a roof over her head and food in the bellies of her children, stumbled upon the same wisdom and announced it in a simpler, more direct Irish proverb: 'A dog owns nothing, but is seldom dissatisfied.'

A satisfied mind is your birthright. When you restore your own factory settings, when you manage to bring your mind back to its default place, you'll find that you're actually happy.

It begins with a simple instruction:

Take a deep breath.

How Does a Bogger Become a Meditation Teacher?

Everyone is a visionary, if you scratch him deep enough. But the Celt, unlike any other, is a visionary without scratching.

— WB YEATS

That's life: starting over, one breath at a time.

— SHARON SALZBERG

I came out of the womb chewing my fingernails. I was born in St Finbar's, Cork, on a wet April morning at the start of the eighties. My father is and was an eternal child, and my mother is and was hopelessly in love with him. I took one look at the pair of them, barely in their twenties, skint and hopeless, naive as parents come, and I knew that I probably shouldn't have selected 'surprise me' off the menu in the waiting room between lives.

We were fairly poor. Not in the romantic, live-off-the-land way; more the tense, nail-biting, where's the rent coming from way. The actor Roberto Benigni won an Oscar in 1998 for the movie *Life Is Beautiful*. In his acceptance speech he thanked his parents for the greatest gift of all: poverty.

This Is It

I'm not saying we had to beg or climb into bins for food, but Santa's gifts never came in their original boxes, rent was something we prayed about and when we visited our cousins they'd say, 'That's my jumper, trousers, shoes …'. We were poor, but in Ireland in the eighties, you didn't have to look far to find someone poorer.

We lived in a caravan in west Cork for the early part of my life. I can't remember many of the details, but I think I can locate the genesis of my residual fear of spiders, the cold and food shortages to that caravan.

We moved to Belfast. My dad took a job back in the city where he came from. Every time there was an explosion outside, he would say 'It's just a car backfiring.' When this excuse wore thin, we packed up and moved south to Raheny in Dublin. For a brief period I can remember my dad wearing silver suits, smelling of cologne and driving a car that might have even been new. If we'd stayed, I could have had the most colourful accent on the whole island, a hybrid mash-up of big city slang and culchie patois, but instead Dad had a burn-out, and we left Dublin and moved to Kildare, where I'd stay for the next fifteen years, and learn to speak in a flat, bogland non-accent: all mutter, no lilt, with my chin never far from my chest. No matter what you asked me, the only thing I could reply with was 'nuthin'.

I can't say I ever felt at home in Kildare, although I am more from Kildare than I am from anywhere else. That county, the flatness of the geography, the schools I went to, the magnetic, soul-sapping pull of the bog, shaped me, in the same way a brass hammer shapes soft metal.

I didn't enjoy my upbringing that much. I got called carrots, I got into lots of fights, I smoked Carroll's cigarettes for about five years and can't remember liking them even once. Aged fourteen, I got traintracks on my teeth and for the next three years, a period that most of my peers would refer to as the 'shifting era', I just opted out of even trying. It's hazy now – in psychology they refer to it as selective recall when we purposely place an obstructive lens around our memories – but I don't think I even got a real shift (tongues, etc.) until I was seventeen. In hindsight these things aren't important, but in the crushing light of teen-agerdom, if you weren't shifting, you weren't really living.

Thich Nhat Hanh is one of the world's most respected meditation teachers. He was nominated for a Nobel Peace Prize for his activism and was a big influence on Martin Luther King Jr, and even Oprah. He has a beautiful phrase that he uses to describe the importance of experiencing struggle: 'No mud, no lotus.' It means that without a little bit of hardship, we never get to truly open our hearts.

Struggle turns into wisdom. Sickness reminds us of the importance of health, heartache teaches us to love, the short, biting days of January help us appreciate the long, balmy month of June. Kildare made me miserable and this made me fall in love with my inner world.

For some years, from maybe when I was six to around twelve, I'd go to sleep every night concentrating on the space inside my head. I would lie there focusing on nothing more than the space between thoughts until stars and lights and flashing trails would appear, and my ears would start ringing. I'd tell my mum, and she'd just smile at me, wondering what new weirdness was coming out of her son's mouth now, but I was actually, bizarrely and intuitively, entering a meditative state known as *samadhi*.

Samadhi is a heightened state of concentration. It's a level of mental absorption that monks spend many hours and even entire lifetimes trying to attain. With no previous experience, I was somehow naturally led to this deep, transformative place. Don't ask me why, it's the only thing that's come naturally to me. Everything else – driving a car, learning languages, sports, instruments, learning to shift, even punctuating the book you're reading right now – has been hard won. It seems like the one unique talent I came into this life with was for zoning out. Although *samadhi*, if we're being really honest, is actually more zoning in. Then when I was twelve my parents bought a TV, and one night home alone I came across *Eurotrash*, and that led me to discover masturbation, and that was the end of my brief experiment with meditation.

I've got no bad feeling towards Kildare, but I grew up in a house where the walls leaked when it rained, I was a target for bullies, and I was too tall to be a jockey, never mind that I was afraid of horses, so by the time I reached seventeen, I left and vowed never to return.

Leaving didn't improve my situation. If you ask god for patience, he'll send you a queue at the bank. I asked god for peace and he sent me a pair of decades with enough drama to fill a screenwriter's library.

In my twenties I experienced lots of depression and anxiety, which in turn propelled me into multiple stormy relationships and a rash of impulsive decisions – somehow, I managed to find myself engaged three times, to three different people, over a five-year period. I become addicted to falling in love, but unlike addictions to substances, mine also involved damaging both myself and another person. I was constantly packing bags, moving out, leaving town, changing address. This meant that for most of my twenties and thirties, my most stable source of income was bar work. Life rarely catches up on you when you work in bars. The barman is the epitome of wisdom, prudence and control, but only because everyone else around him is in tatters. I could dispense advice and wisdom when they were listening and strong-arm them through the door by the time they couldn't any more.

My problems were clear to me. I had chronic anxiety, and a unique capacity for finding the negativity in everything.

There's a phenomenon known as bog apathy. It's an attitude I grew up swimming in. You don't go to the doctor if you're sick. You don't get further education if you're ambitious. You don't try to change your life for the better because there's no point. You resign yourself to never getting anywhere because the opportunities seem so limited. Depending on where you lived, or what your parents did, you could have a trace of it or a full-blown outbreak.

'You're on Earth. There's no cure for that,' said Samuel Beckett, possibly referring to the part of Kildare I knew. Like a lot of the people I grew up with, we just didn't picture much positive coming towards us, and so we attracted none. I couldn't manage a relationship for longer than two months. I drank often, and I often drank alone. I was insomniac on and off, and I was never really happy, but then I didn't expect to be. My workaround was to chase after any flickering excitement that came my way. This made me reckless and impulsive. Between eighteen and maybe twenty-eight, I can't remember saying no to a drug.

But one time, being impulsive actually worked for me. I signed up for a ten-day silent meditation retreat for a laugh. From 4 a.m. until 10.30 p.m., in one-hour intervals, for ten solid days, I sat cross-legged in a big draughty room in the mountains of Italy while a tinny recording gave instructions on how to observe the breath. Oh lord, it was hell. My legs ached, my butt felt like it was on fire and my mind, a place I'd barely explored, was a never-ending collage of regrets, wants and realisations that came at me like headbutts in a dark corridor.

It was like a lifetime of therapy every single day, and it was too much for me to take. I tried to leave, but a very kind Italian teacher suggested I stay just another day. 'What have you got to lose?' What a great question. In most circumstances when we're asked it, we really don't have that much.

I acquiesced. I walked into the hall, I sat down and within just a few breaths, I'd found myself in the same meditative state I'd known as a child. For the first time in nearly twenty years I felt calm, and I started crying. For three more days, I meditated and I cried, as wave after wave of sadness and joy washed over me. And when the last day came, and we all started talking again, and the only language around me was Italian, I made a decision to commit myself to meditation.

Buddha. My man. You had me at *namaste*.

David Lynch, the movie director, is also a meditator. He said this: 'The thing about meditation is: you become more and more you.' After my first experience with meditation, I decided to become more me. I decided to get to know the person behind all the tall stories. Here's the thing. The energy that you put into your own self-destruction can also be put into your own construction. The best meditators I've met were the worst messers before they started.

I took myself off to India and lived in a monastery. I stayed with monks in the Californian desert. I studied in San Francisco with the same people who'd brought mindfulness to Silicon Valley. I read every sky-blue-covered book on spirituality, and then I came back to Ireland to be with my sick father while, high on morphine, he raindanced with dream warriors who visited him in the intensive care ward of St James's every night.

That was a decision I hadn't expected to have to make. When I discovered my dad was ill, I just dropped everything and came home. It was one of the easiest decisions I'd ever made. But really not one that I ever thought I would make.

Here's a warning: if you start meditating you will also start surprising yourself.

While I was home, I got offered a housesit in Clare. One day I went into Limerick City and ran into an old friend who was working with men who'd just been released from prison. They were trying to piece their lives back together and she was helping them. We talked and I told her about meditation, and then she asked me if I'd teach them. I said yes. And again, it was one of the easiest decisions I'd ever made.

I was scared and underprepared, but sometimes in life, all the gears start turning at once. This happens when you fall in love. When you migrate. When someone or something dies. When a pandemic grips the planet. The numerous competing voices in our head are funnelled into one, clear question: what needs to be done right now?

So I decided to teach the course, despite not really feeling ready to teach meditation, and I credit that with being the catalyst behind my life as a teacher.

The first day we met as a group, I had to put my hands between my legs because they were shaking as I spoke.

Shaky hands are not a good look on a meditation teacher. I felt intimidated; teaching men who were my own age and from my own country brought me back to all my childhood vulnerability. They smoked Carroll's, and if you asked them what they did at the weekend, they might give you an answer, but they might also just say 'nuthin'.

We met once a week in a cold block-shaped building on the river. The men who came along had known tough lives. I thought I had; but perspective is everything. In middle-class circles where no one's gone to bed hungry, I can play my tiny violin, but compared to my group in Limerick I may as well have been born with a silver spoon in my gob. Many of them came from Moyross or the Island. They all smoked, school-gate style, into their hands, on the stoop of the building, and they welcomed me like a family member.

Inside the building was as loud as a tambourine. You heard every conversation on the street, every diesel engine charging along the quays, every time a council worker mooched by with a garden strimmer and his slacks sliding down his arse. But we also had silence, and the silence in that space, with ten men, cups of tea with the bags in, Mikado biscuits gone in ten seconds, a Dimplex pouring out gassy heat in the corner, was so profound you could hear the sound of a tracksuit rubbing against a leg.

For a little over a month, we'd sit and meditate upstairs in a common room and then the men would go down to a factory space and learn how to solder, how to weld, how to carve wood into useful objects. I didn't know the details but I knew that most of these guys had grown up in worlds that made mine seem like a bed of daisies.

At the end of my time teaching there something happened. One of the men came up to me and said, 'You know what? We've stopped listening to the radio. We used to have the radio on all the time, but since we started meditating, we all just started to like the silence more. We never put the tunes on any more. It's lovely.'

After nearly all our sessions, I left the building, turned the corner onto George's Quay and cried. I feel so grateful to those men for allowing me to show them what I knew about meditation, and for taking me seriously.

Meditation is very simple, but it's also really hard. You've got to go into it with no expectation, even though you're obviously trying it for a reason. You've got to make some effort, but not too much. You've got to let go without dropping completely off to sleep. You need to be determined but not grasp. You need to want it, but you also need to not want anything at all. Meditation is very simple, but it's also really hard, and after an entire lifetime you'll still feel like a beginner.

Many students tell me, 'Oh, I can't meditate' or 'It's not for me,' but the reality is if you've got thought in your head and breath in your body, you can meditate. So if you do in fact have breath in your body, and the simplest way to check is to hold a page in front of your nose and see if it moves, you can do it.

'Your feet will bring you where your heart wants to go' is something my Irish teacher used to tell us when she found us milling around in the hallway, late for class. She was right, we had no interest in being near the classroom, our hearts wanted to go anywhere but there, but I hope for both our sakes that you've a little more interest in meditation, so let's go on.

Exercise: The breath

You can start wherever you are. Sitting on a bus. At home on your bed. Even on the loo. You don't need to climb a mountain or shave your head, or give up sex and alcohol. You can be an unhealthy, angry, slobby mess and still meditate. We take all comers. The only requirement is that you can breathe, and that you're somehow willing.

Very simply, close your eyes and bring your attention to the breath in your body.

There are three main areas where you can feel the breath: the nose, the chest and the belly. So whichever one feels best to you right now, just pay attention to that.

Do this for a short while every day. You can set a timer. Five minutes is a good number to start with.

Every time you notice that you're not doing it, start again.

Spoiler Alert: You will notice you're not doing it almost all the time. Don't stress about that. This is just the nature of the mind. When it's not trained, it's very hard to pay attention. It's like telling a puppy to sit. The likely response is that they'll just go chew your socks. The untrained mind is a lot like an untrained puppy. You need to be patient. You also need to be gentle. But by doing this exercise for some minutes every day you'll slowly build up attention stamina.

Learning to pay attention to what you want to, rather than what's just appearing in your mind, or in the world around you, is the number one thing you can do to improve the quality of your life.

Meditation can be difficult. Don't worry. This is why we call it a practice.

What Happens when You're Away with the Fairies?

You will never plough a field by turning it over in your mind.

— IRISH PROVERB

The goal of meditation isn't to control your thoughts, it's to stop letting them control you.

— DAN MILLMAN

Something happened to me when I turned ten. I think it happens to a lot of boys. We begin to change. Spots started appearing across my chin, hair sprouted around my genitals and my thoughts transformed from the usual childhood wonder at each living, shining, banal thing to falling in love.

Overnight I went from the kind of kid who wanted to know all about the mysteries of the Irish countryside, to put a name to every bug, tree and bird, to a weird, spotty, asocial creature who stayed in his room with the curtains closed and the lights off, fantasising about falling in love. We never talked about romance, or even sex, in my house. To be honest, I didn't know any families who did. I have a couple of friends from back home who both got pregnant when they were only teenagers. Their parents asked them, 'How did you let a thing like that happen?' They replied, 'Because you never told us how to not make it happen.'

Between third and fifth year in school, about six girls in my class dropped out because, as it was explained to us by our year head, they'd suddenly become pregnant. Like they'd suddenly become cold, suddenly become ill, suddenly become bored, suddenly become famous. Teenage pregnancies where I grew up were very short on detail. Probably because the older people thought that if we knew the details we'd all get pregnant.

Buddha said that if there were a stronger energy than sexual energy in the world, nobody would ever get enlightened. And I wholeheartedly agree with the guy, but I feel that with me, the waters were muddier than that. I wasn't a ten-year-old dying to get laid; I was a ten-year-old dying to be in love. The next part is a little bit cringe, so if you'd like, now's a good time to take a deep breath.

I had a notebook with the top ten girls I had crushes on. Some were in school. Some I'd only met once or twice; and one, a girl I described in my notebook as 'blue hat girl', I'd only ever seen from the back seat of a car that passed by our front door while I was outside on the street playing kerbs. Each morning I'd wake up, pick one girl, and then spend the day imagining that I was with her instead of all the other things that I was actually doing. It was like an imaginary friend, only I had ten of them and they worked a schedule. Of course, I never actually talked to any of them. I was too shy to make it real. Edel, Tracey, Samantha, Maedbh – did you even know? The fantasy of being in love and being loved was enough.

By the age of eleven, the thing I was best at was being lost in my own fantasy world. I think many kids are. I was not happy in my home. Being a kid, I couldn't exactly leave, but I could try to get as far away from it as possible while still being in it. I got some sheets of chipboard, laid them out across the rafters and moved into the attic. I moved away from my family because my hormones felt like an embarrassing affliction, but also because the years of listening to my parents argue had got to me.

The attic, like attics in all run-down homes, was full of spiders. There were corners of that space where their webs were thick enough to balance a book on. I have always had a deep fear of spiders. It began when I was a toddler and a daddy longlegs ran right across my face, or so my sister told me. A few Christmases back I found myself north of San Francisco working on a weed farm. There were some

This Is It

lovely people there. We all lived and worked in houses, caravans and old barns dotted around the property. There were dogs and cats too. It felt like a commune, only we were trimming and bagging illegal marijuana. The other trimmers came from the San Francisco queer and hippy scenes. Gentle, kind folk. I suppose I'd imagined myself as the strong man among them. I don't know why, I'm really not, but we invent roles for ourselves sometimes when we believe in everything that we think. Anyway, over Christmas we were sitting down on sofas and the floor in the big living room watching *Home Alone* and eating sweet popcorn, and you know that scene where the tarantula crawls across Joe Pesci? Well, it came up and I let out a squeal. And everyone looked at me like I was a small child.

To this day, I don't fully understand how I could handle being up in that attic space surrounded by so many creepy crawlies, but I guess it speaks to how difficult it was for me to be around my family, and how strong my capacity for living in a fantasy world had become.

I'd climb back down at mealtimes, and while my family peppered me with questions, I'd just stare at my plate and ignore them. 'He's away with the fairies' my mother would say. But if we'd invited a therapist for dinner, they would have said, 'No, Mrs Creighton, your boy is actually depressed. He's disengaging from the world around him because it's a place of overwhelming stress and anxiety, where the children have adopted parental roles. Cheque, please!'

We spend almost fifty per cent of our time in stimulus-free thought or, as some would say, lost in thought, and as others would say, being away with the fairies. And while spending time with small people who can fly and have a wicked sense of humour would be awesome, we know from scientific data that the overwhelming majority of our thoughts are not the fairy kind, they're actually the miserable kind. As much as eighty per cent of our thoughts can be classified as negative – that is, associated with worry, stress, regret and anxious planning.

The next sentence is important, so I'm writing it in bold: **Our brains are not designed to make us happy, they're designed to keep us alive.**

The brain you're using to read this is the latest model of a version that was designed over 200,000 years ago. Back then, when we lived in caves and were surrounded by things that wanted to eat us, it was important that this brain was constantly attuned to potential danger, because the world was packed with danger. Long-fanged animals, poisonous plants, the threat of starvation.

What that means today, in an age when there aren't any tigers trying to get us, is that our brains are still constantly on the look-out for danger. Your brain is like a small dog barking at the slightest sound, regardless of whether it's a friend, a stranger, or just the wind against a door. The habit of your brain is to find a problem and funnel all your attention to that problem. With no lions, leopards or tigers chasing you down on your daily commute, it casts around for other problems: your finances, your love life, your appearance, your health. How much time have you lost looking in the mirror worrying that you're looking older? You can thank your problem-seeking brain for that.

I may have been lost in fantasy through half of my adolescent life, but the other half of the time I was neck deep in worries that operated like air raid sirens inside my head. School was frightening. Every class felt like walking out on a stage. What if you call the teacher Mum, instead of Ms? What if you get asked to go to the board? What if you get an erection and it won't subside and you've somehow got to get out of the room bent double with nobody noticing?

The brain is extremely good at what it does. Nothing keeps you on your toes like a brain. Most of us go through our entire lives without realising just how little we're in control of them. Most people think they're driving. When you begin to meditate, one of the first things you see is that yes, you're in the driving seat, but you've been so busy tuning the radio and playing with the A/C that you haven't touched the steering wheel in a thousand miles.

In Zen they have a saying that the first step on the path is to realise the madness of your own thoughts. If you're reading this and you can recognise truth in this, it's no reason to panic. We all start off this way. We're all messy at the beginning.

The next step is to realise that you're actually creating the conditions for these thoughts. This is tough. It means taking the blame for so many things you've been trying to outsource. Your pride can take a real walloping at this stage. This is a good thing. Pride is ego. That will take a walloping too.

The third step is to become so stable that when thoughts enter your mind, it's like a thief breaking into an empty house. There's nothing for them to steal. When thoughts enter the head of a very experienced meditator they've nowhere to stick. This is liberation. You still get thoughts but they don't hang around because you don't hang on to them. Imagine that. This is total awareness and we're capable of it if we practise. Once you can see for yourself that your thoughts are nothing more than constantly changing phenomena, you can choose which ones to pay attention to. What a relief, right? Ordinarily, it's like intergalactic cable television in there, with no censorship, no quality control and no shame in showing re-runs over and over again. Really, if we humans externalised rather than internalised our thoughts, nobody would get a second date on this planet again.

A lot of people come to my classes, and in the beginning when we're doing a round of introductions, I'll say, 'Tell me why you're here,' and they'll often reply, 'I want to switch off my thoughts.' I'll say, 'Well, I have some bad news for you. Before we learn to switch the thoughts off, we're going to start by switching them on full blast.' And then their eyes get big. And I say, 'Don't worry, it'll get worse before it gets better.'

And this is the exercise we do.

Exercise: Who's in control of your mind?

Sit anyway you like but preferably somewhere quiet, preferably somewhere you won't be disturbed by your housemate or your partner or your cat. Believe it or not, animals are drawn to meditators like they're drawn to sunspots.

I can't tell you how many times I've opened my eyes to find a dog or a cat curled up next to me at the end of my meditation.

Now choose a celebrity. It can be any celebrity. But because this is my book, I'm going to choose Michael D. Higgins as an example. Get an image of Michael D. in your mind. Then set a timer on your phone for one minute. Close your eyes, and for the entirety of that minute just focus on Michael D.

So how was that?

If you're like most people you'll have managed to keep your focus on Michael D. for a few seconds and then your mind got dragged into random thoughts. Ask yourself the following questions regarding those random thoughts.

Did you plan to think about them?

Did they surprise you?

Why was it so hard to focus on Michael D.?

This is just a short exercise to illustrate how we're not always in charge of what goes on in our minds. We don't get to decide what thought comes up next, in the same way you don't get to decide what sentence I write next.

Have you ever obsessed over something to the point where it drove you nuts?

Have you ever made yourself sick with worry?

Have you ever been so horribly depressed, so flooded with dark, mean thoughts that you couldn't get out of bed for days?

I used to get anxiety attacks that were so bad the only thing I could do was curl up in a ball on the carpet. I've experienced depression that kept me in bed for days. I can remember being at a house party – I don't know how it happens, but even when you're depressed, you can still end up at parties – and it sticks in my head, the way all the worst things do: one minute I was in a conversation with someone, and the next they were standing up, apologising and saying, 'I'm sorry, pal, you're just so heavy.' Reader, they were right. I was heavy with thoughts. The good news is that change is possible, and it begins when you recognise that it's your thoughts that are pulling the strings. When you meditate, you're not stopping the thoughts, you're just *remembering* there's an alternative to thinking. The alternative is to keep your focus on the breath and not get tangled in thoughts.

I'll end this chapter with a very useful piece of advice. It's the kind of advice I wish my grandmother had given me, but she didn't: **Don't believe everything you think.**

Up to 90

To live is the rarest thing in the world. Most people exist, that is all.

— OSCAR WILDE

Using a camera appeases the anxiety which the work-driven feel about not working when they are on vacation.

— SUSAN SONTAG

It's not easy being a human. We've been designed with many significant flaws. Our skin bruises very easily. We need to eat every day. As far as predators go, we're not exactly fierce. Our teeth and nails aren't frightening anybody. Some of us can't even sit in the hot sun for more than a few hours without becoming pink and woozy. But the most significant flaw we have, and it's no doubt the reason you've read so much of this book already, is our brains. For all the wonderful computational, conceptual magic they can perform, they're very hard to control. This is frustrating.

Our brains are incredible devices. They are, as far as we know and we already know so much, the most sophisticated thing in the whole universe. Imagine that. We have

24/7, VIP, Access All Areas privileges to the most incredible device ever known. But these devices are assembled with one major glitch: our neural activity increases for automatic stimulus and decreases for the things we're actually paying attention to. This is why it's hard to focus and might explain why it's hard to get through a chapter of this book, or any book for that matter, without responding to the pings coming from your phone.

It all comes down to focus. The brain has two ways of focusing: top down and bottom up. Top-down focus is when you're looking at a map, or a work of art, or a view across a sprawling valley. Bottom-up focus is when a dog barks, or tyres screech, or a fire engine buzzes by. Anything that stands out from the usual will command our focus. I'm trying my hardest to keep you on the page here but I know that all it's going to take is a car radio on the street, or a door opening in the next room, and I've lost you. In fact, all I have to do is say the word 'phone' and you might want to look at it. It's probably beside you, whispering softly, gently, 'You know you want to.'

It's no fluke that the social media gods gave notifications the colour red. A red dot on a screen is irresistible to the human brain in the same way that Jägerbomb rounds are irresistible to hen parties. I know this for a fact. I have probably more experience as a barman than as a meditation teacher. If you're old enough, I might even have served you. I might have made the Jägerbomb that ruined your weekend. This book is my penance.

So this is your brain. It's designed to respond to distractions. And this isn't a bad thing. If there is actually a fire engine outside your door, it's probably safest that you do pull your nose out of this book and check that they're not coming to your house. Let's not completely bash this response. It's the thing that's kept our species alive for so long. We can see, sense and even smell danger. But when we become a slave to all the distractions and all the impulses, and all the imagined dangers, it can turn our lives into a living misery.

I had a friend who worked as an emergency dispatcher in Las Vegas. The job was so rapid, so stressful and so demanding, and the worst part is you never ever find out if the call gets resolved. You just move on to the next break-in, house fire, heart attack. Nobody tells you. She left after a couple of years and became a croupier at the Golden Nugget, and then a break-up or two later she ended up, as many of us do, in therapy, and after therapy she attended a silent meditation retreat. Her insight after this retreat was something that you might find true too: her inner monologue, she said, was like being an emergency dispatcher again, only this time with no days off, no lunchbreaks, and fielding multiple calls at once. For most of us life is a dance between emergencies, and this is why most of us are always tired.

I played football for the under tens in Sallins. It was, in hindsight, probably the peak of my sporting career. We were in the seventh division, which meant that most of the other teams we played against were tiny parishes way out in the bog who could just about field fifteen players but often lacked basic things like nets for their goals, or enough matching bibs for the whole team. Sometimes they took to the field with girls making up the number. That was always a bit of a shock.

We didn't know how to mark girls. In fairness, we didn't know anything about them either. We weren't meant to. My mother ran a playschool in the front of our house, and I started off with lots of girl friends. Some were my neighbours. We'd play together after school. On my first day of primary school, another boy told me that you're not supposed to do that.

'Boys don't play with girls, did you not know that?'

I didn't but I stopped. I think he must have told all the boys in the whole school because we all stopped playing with girls that same week.

So we didn't know much about girls and playing football against them felt kind of unnerving. What if we touched one in a tackle, would that mean we'd have to go out with them for ever, and get married, move to Kinnegad, turn her people into our people?

Complicated gender politics aside, we won every game we played that season. I even managed to score own goals in two games, and we still won. But this didn't satisfy our trainer. He could find problems in everything. A long, long time before smartphones and social media, his world was one of bright red notifications that needed to be dealt with immediately. On the bus to and from games, he'd roam up and down the aisle, displacing boys here and there so he could take a seat and individually berate our performances.

'Creighton, you gave your man a two-yard start for that 45. Do you think you have wings for feet?'

'No.'

'And where'd you learn to bounce a ball, the dark side of the feckin' moon?'

We all got the impression that he cared more about the games than we did. A lot more. Adults who train kids are often like this. I don't know, but I can't help but think that kids probably wouldn't learn to compete so much if it weren't for angry adults telling them they had to.

To be fair, some of us only played to get out of classes. None of us ever wanted to play in the rain or the cold, and it was hard for us to buy into his pre-game rallying cry: 'Are you ready to die for Sallins?' when many of us hated Sallins, and wished we'd been born in Naas. That season we qualified for division six, and over the summer, less than two weeks into the holidays, our trainer had a heart attack and was told by the doctor he could never go back to training under-tens Gaelic football again.

Growing up, all our dads seemed to have heart attacks in their fifties. We had the language to describe them – coronary thrombosis, congestive heart failure, cardiac infarction, aneurysm – before we even had the language to describe the emotions flooding our wimpy, pre-pubescent bodies. Having a heart attack felt like it was a rite of passage amongst men. You finished school, you got a job, you married, had a kid and then ended up in hospital. Our role models were men who were so busy that they eventually made themselves sick. Our mothers weren't really that different. They operated like 24-hour corner stores in big cities – their lights never went out. They never seemed to sit. Our mothers hovered, their arms always full of washing, or dishes, or their lost and swollen dreams. So many of the grown-ups around us were up to 90. So many of them operated at levels you wouldn't expect of a high-performance motor. So many of them ended up in hospital.

Many people come to meditation after a burn-out. A doctor will tell them to go home and do nothing, and they'll think this advice is sound, coming from a trained medical professional and all, but then they'll get home and start throwing themselves into projects, and housework, and dry-lining the spare room, until a second visit to the hospital will confirm that maybe they don't actually know how to do nothing. Maybe they can't stop themselves. If I don't resist the urge to be busy, I could work all day long. Nearly every single one of us is like this.

The hardest part of meditation is the doing nothing. The language we use to explain the technique is so simple it almost sounds patronising, but doing nothing, practising doing nothing, is the key to meditation.

The journey can't begin unless you're prepared to stop for a minute. We spend so much of our lives doing something that it's only when we do nothing that we realise how agitated we are. I always liken it to the feeling of loneliness that would hit whenever I left a busy pub.

I'd walk out and as the noise faded behind me, it'd be replaced by feelings of how isolated I was in the world. I worked in bars for so many years, and it's a great profession for travelling and collecting stories, but all bar workers – and I know this is a broad stroke, so let's say most long-termers rather than all bartenders – are deeply lonely individuals. We're the watchmen of the night. At the party but not a part of the party. Kings of small talk, founts of jokes, phenomenal aggregators of horse racing, football and election results. But we end our shifts when the streets are quiet. We eat the sandwiches that you leave behind in Centra: tuna, egg mayo, tomato salad on a bap. And we sleep through all the beautiful mornings with black-out blinds or eye masks. Your local barman or barwoman may be surly, but that's only because they're probably also pretty sad.

There's a reason many of us operate at 90 mph. It's a tried and trusted method for avoiding yourself and avoiding the bad feelings at our core. Burn-outs and heart attacks are the body's way of telling you that you can't do that for ever. Jon Kabat-Zinn, the legendary meditation teacher, wrote a book all about that exact topic. He called it *Wherever You Go, There You Are*. It too has a sky-blue cover. The premise of the book is very simple. Simplicity is key with meditation. If you ask me, I think the simplicity is what some people find annoying. It sounds patronising.

But basically it's this – you can't escape yourself indefinitely. At some stage you'll have to stop and say, 'Okay, this is me, let's talk.'

Men have a habit of avoiding the question, 'How are you?' We tend to answer obliquely.

'Oh, you know, not doing much, just pottering about.'

'But how are you?'

'Yeah, bits and pieces, keeping busy.'

'You're not listening. I said, "How are you?"'

'Sure, you know yourself.'

I wrote this book as a way of confronting the expression 'Sure, you know yourself.' We use it to shut down a conversation about ourselves. We use it as a language place holder when no real emotional, vulnerable alternative is available. If we were being totally honest we wouldn't say, 'Sure, you know yourself,' we'd say, 'Shit, I don't even know how to begin to communicate this to you, can we just drop it?' I don't blame us for all being so busy and for not answering the serious questions. We've created a society where economic growth is more important than personal growth.

It's not just men who are guilty of not answering this question. All of us have the habit of ignoring what's really going on with ourselves. What are we so afraid of? Why do we place so much value on being so busy? And what would actually happen if we were to finally stop?

If we were to stop, we'd discover that there are parts of us that we can't stand to be around. But your job as a human is to do just that. Your job as a human is to accept yourself, and all your many broken, bruised and unloved parts. This is how we transform.

Exercise: What's making you go so fast?

As we talked about earlier, you don't have to believe all your thoughts. They are really just a product of the environment you find yourself in. And while you might believe this at a theoretical level, integrating this truth is extremely hard. Each thought that appears arrives like a screaming child demanding your attention. This is the nature of thoughts. They are incredibly persistent. Maybe you've noticed? Maybe you've had a song stuck in your head, or an argument or a limiting thought that's been with you for a while. Maybe it's been with you your entire life?

These thoughts play out like a radio in the background on a factory floor. Only, unlike the radio that nobody really listens to, the thoughts in your head are subconsciously influencing everything you do. They're the ones in the driving seat, and when you're unhappy there's a very good chance they're the culprit. Unconscious thoughts are the soundtrack to all our lives.

A way to understand what soundtrack is playing in the background of your life is to get in the habit of writing down what thoughts you've had that day. Before you go to bed, or on your lunch break, or as they appear throughout the day. You'll notice something: thoughts are repetitive and they are overwhelmingly negative, and we give them way too much power over us.

By recognising our thoughts, which ones keep appearing, we're bringing them out of the shadows and into a place where they can't hurt us the same way. This is how healing works. This is how you change a life.

Have a notebook next to you. Use the margin of this book, even. And every day make a note of the headline thoughts that have been playing their greatest hits in your brain.

Stop the Lights

To gain that which is worth having, it may be necessary to lose everything else.

— BERNADETTE DEVLIN

The answer lies within ourselves. If we can't find peace and happiness there, it's not going to come from the outside.

— TENZIN PALMO

Sometimes it can take a global pandemic to make us stop. Generally it takes something bigger than ourselves. Our habits, or more accurately our inability to see how they are shaping our lives, are so strong that we can be powerless to do anything about it until there's an intervention. Emergencies, catastrophes, illnesses, unexpected break-ups and pandemics are all interventions, the rare but expected moments when life forces us to do what we lack the courage to do on our own.

When I first moved to Los Angeles, I was very lonely, so I joined an AA group in Venice Beach. I didn't have a strong meditation practice at this stage, or I would have just joined a spiritual community. Venice Beach Alcoholics

Anonymous were a pretty wild group. At the end of every meeting, after the Lord's Prayer, they gave a surf report for the coming week, and then we all filed into the hallway to drink filter coffee and smoke vapes. Many of them lived in RVs at the beach. Some of them lived on ramshackle boats in the cheap marinas. Often when you'd fall into conversation with them, they'd tell you a story about how a medical bill had put them out of their home, or they were on the run from a whole gang of credit card companies. When I first arrived in LA, I was in the habit of asking people how they were. But I hadn't expected they'd really tell me. A total stranger might corral you for ten minutes if you smiled at them. All cities are lonely, but LA is lonely in a uniquely painful way.

I didn't really have a classic drink problem. I used alcohol primarily as a crutch in social situations. I was shy, so any birthdays, dinners, events and, later, when I got a little success, book readings, required alcohol. I couldn't have gone on a date without it. Certainly couldn't have hooked up with someone. At least not the first few times. I can remember going on a date in my twenties with a girl who didn't drink. She watched me go through a bottle of wine and try to hold a conversation, with great patience, and then she never called me again.

My dad and his brother were both alcoholics, so I always imagined that I would become one too, but for some reason, call it grace, when I needed to stop, I could. The men I met at AA could only stop when they hit a wall. They had all ended up there because of some kind of intervention. Some had lost jobs. Some had done jail time. All of them – each last, sun-bleached one of them – had lost someone they loved because of their drinking. One guy, Charlie, had been a dentist in Colorado who'd managed to continue to practise with shaky hands for years until he got found out.

'What did it in the end, Charlie?'

'I took out the wrong tooth.'

'I'm sure that happens all the time.'

'I did it to the same person twice.'

'Shit, Charlie.'

'When I lost the practice, I lost my wife and then, well, it was just too painful to try and see my daughter once a week, so I moved away altogether. I've grandkids now. We FaceTime now and then, but my daughter only lets me talk to them if I'm going to the meetings. She won't listen to another excuse or another relapse. I've run out of road.'

Many people don't stop until they run out of road. Personally, if I'd had a little bit more success as a novelist and got the fame I was craving, or maybe if I'd managed to fall in love and actually stay in love, I'd probably never have stopped either. The discomfort needs to reach a certain level before we decide to attend to it. Oftentimes, the first step to happiness is depression, anxiety, loneliness, heartache, all the bad guys. These are our body's way of forcing an intervention, telling us we've run out of road and it's time to stop.

If you're going through a rough time now, it can be good to remember that rough times always precede good times. Them's the rules. A lot of people come to meditation because they want to stop, or because they've become stuck. They're both the same thing, actually.

My mother did everything at home. For a while, she was not only the breadwinner, she was also the breadmaker. She was always on the go. She got up before any of us and came home after all of us, and was still expected to make dinner, feed the dog, help us with our homework and act as a one-person United Nations peace-keeping mission between my sister and my dad, and occasionally my sister and me. I was the baby in the house. It used to frustrate me so much that my mother wouldn't spend the time to forensically investigate the numerous arguments between my sister and me, instead of just dismissing it with 'It takes two to tango.'

But I get it now. She was just exhausted and racing against a ticking clock all day long. When I think back on all the kitchens I walked through as a kid, and all the mothers who fed me and told me to leave my mucky football boots at the back door, they were all exhausted.

There's an expression that you hear all the time if you listen to spiritual podcasts or attend spiritual talks and whatnot. It's hackneyed, but with no better alternatives presenting themselves, it'll have to do: Put on your own oxygen mask before assisting others. So many of us don't heed this simple instruction, and so many of us wouldn't even know where to begin to heed it. We have brains that function in such a way that if we're not careful, we might not even consider taking care of ourselves until it's too late. Our brains are not designed to prioritise our bliss, they're designed to prioritise our productivity. As much as we might externalise our problems and blame others for the situations we find ourselves in, I'm sorry to say it, but we're our own biggest enemy.

Nobody has the power to make you feel as good or as bad as you do.

There are two ways in which people don't stop: one is by ignoring their own needs through addiction; and the other is ignoring their own needs by putting themselves last. Both are situations where self-worth and self-love are in short supply.

One of the kindest things you can do for yourself is to stop. The amazing thing about stopping is that once you've done it, you begin to see how much clearer things are. It's the equivalent of a slap across the face. The way we stop in meditation is by making a switch from doing to being. Animals operate like this – at least the ones who haven't been selectively bred into complete neurosis. They're in the moment. Small children too. They can cry, then laugh with very little transition time. It's as if things don't stick to them. We grown-ups are the opposite. It's like we're made of Velcro.

You know when you go to the sea, when you walk along Brittas or Inch, or even Tramore? There's a magical moment that happens. It's brief and it's very subtle, but this is why we go to the beach in the first place. It's why we climb mountains, and take walks in woods and throw ourselves in the sea on freezing mornings in March: nature is so powerful that it actually changes our mindset. When we're immersed in the awesome beauty of nature, we switch from doing to just being. It's why we like dogs. Yes, they get us out of the house and their love is guaranteed, until perhaps the day we keel over in the kitchen and they eventually eat us, but the real reason we love dogs is because they too, like Clew Bay, Lahinch Beach and even Howth Harbour, have the power to take us out of doing and into being.

The problem with stopping is that you have to do it yourself. When I go home, I watch my mother respond to every phone call, every text message – each alert an ear-blistering scream because she has the volume set to jackhammer. I want to tell her to stop, that she doesn't need to answer every message; but the desire to stop has to come from yourself. She does eventually, but she's spent her life feeling responsible for others and that's not a habit that you just drop. The same goes for relaxing. When in the history of the entire human race has one homo sapiens said to another, 'Will ye relax' and it actually worked?

When we meditate for five, ten, however minutes every day we're training ourselves to get better at stopping. And at the start, just like your first spin class, your first time getting on a treadmill, or even your first time lying flat on a weights bench, it can be depressingly clear that you're really not very good at this. As junk wisdom as this sounds, it takes a lot of skill to do a lot of nothing.

I met a Buddhist called Tenzin Palmo in the Himalayas. I sought her out because I'd heard so much about her. Other folks I'd met at monasteries in northern India had told me that she was a living *arahant*. An *arahant* is someone who has gained insight into the true nature of existence and reached nirvana. It's a pretty big deal. If you're an *arahant* you don't advertise it, and it's taboo to claim it – Tenzin Palmo had not – but there was a whole lot of buzz around her.

She'd spent over a year in a cave meditating on her own. She slept for only three hours a night and even then, she'd sleep upright, lucid dreaming, entirely aware of her mind. This happens on retreat sometimes. You just stop sleeping. You go to bed and lie there. It's spooky at first, but then you get up the next day feeling rested anyway, so you forget about it. Tenzin Palmo forgot about it for a year. She was an Olympic-level stopper. When I met her, she had this kind of surreal presence about her that made it hard to form words, so I didn't ask her much, but she told me that the only reason she started again was because an Indian policeman had climbed the hill to her cave and asked to see her visa, which had expired, so they deported her.

And she told me this: 'The more you realise, the more you realise there is nothing to realise.' The idea that there's somewhere we have got to get to, and something we have to attain, is our basic delusion.

A lot of people who don't know how to stop are living under a basic delusion. The delusion is that the world will stop spinning if we stop moving. Or the delusion is that if we don't respond to each and every panicked thought we'll somehow fall to pieces. Our thoughts and worries are like Tamagotchis. Remember them? They were the original attention-suckers. We cared for them with an intensity that made no sense. The same can be said of our thoughts. Meditation is our way of waking up from this behaviour. It's our way of making the radical decision to stop now and again. And when we stop, when we don't take that call, when we don't fix the next problem, when we don't go after the next job, the next like, the next impulse, we find that the stopping makes the going that follows it significant and profound and deliberate and deeply beautiful.

Exercise: Stopping

Try it now.

Put the book down on your lap and close your eyes. Don't set a timer, don't plan your stopping, just stop for however long you need. Don't try to get anywhere, don't try to achieve anything, don't have any expectations, just stop. You will feel all kinds of impulses to begin again. Your mind will become full with stimulation, but just resist it, if only for a minute or two.

It's a radical thing to do.

It's a radical thing to give yourself permission to do nothing.

Our brains are not trained for this, and yours will most likely revolt pretty quickly, but just watching the impulses and ignoring them briefly is an incredibly courageous act.

Stopping is scary.

I've taken many great lessons from gurus, teachers and wise folks at bus stops, but when it comes to stopping, giving yourself permission to rest, I doff my hat to the house cats of this world.

So right now, in the style of your favourite tabby, moggie or ginger, just stop the lights and be.

Getting a Grip

The long gaze back is always turned inward.
— MAEVE BRENNAN

Welcome the present moment as if you had invited it. Why? Because it is all we ever have.
— PEMA CHÖDRÖN

When I was a teenager I became very uncomfortable with silence. From the minute I came home from school, I'd go to my room and play music. I listened to a lot of nineties grunge. Now, I know there was some uplifting grunge bands back then. You had the Pixies, or even Jane's Addiction and the Breeders and what have you, bands you could conceivably listen to at the gym, on sunny days, cleaning the house and so on, but I preferred the really miserable grunge: the Smashing Pumpkins, the unplugged Nirvana sessions, Alice in Chains' 'Down in a Hole' played on a copied cassette until the plastic tape had worn thin and spat smoke out of the cassette drive. The more depressing it was, the more I liked it. I often fell asleep listening to this music. And when I finally got a stereo with a continual loop function I began waking up to music too.

When I left home, I travelled and found myself working in bars and clubs where the music was so loud I'd hear it in my ears hours after going to bed. I lived with DJs and my homes were always soundtracked with drum 'n' bass and hip hop beats. This suited me, as it suits many of us. I didn't like silence. Silence spooked me. I didn't like to be in a room with no noise. I was always turning on televisions, pressing play, turning a tuner to Lyric FM or talk radio, anything. I think a lot of people are like this. I've stayed in so many houses where something is always on.

Many of us are plagued by the thoughts that appear when we're silent. When we stop distracting ourselves from the discomfort and tune into this silence, the thoughts get louder and louder. Loud thoughts are less fun than experimental dentistry. Some people would rather do away with themselves altogether than listen to the loud thoughts in their mind.

By meditating we're finding ways to accommodate the many parts of ourselves, the sadness, the pain and the worry. It's not magic, it's just a very simple way of accepting who we are in our entirety, and the only way to do this is to stop distracting ourselves. Silence is the ultimate buzz kill. It's the equivalent of all the lights coming on at the end of a disco. Silence means it's time to go home, it's time to face yourself.

The problem many of us have with meditation is the silence. But the silence is crucial. You'll never get to know yourself if you don't get to know yourself in silence. When we begin to explore the silence, the first thing we notice is that our minds are not quite in tune – they're either slightly hyper or slightly depressed. The instinctive urge when confronted with this truth is to either get up and stop meditating or to begin striving to change this. This is a trap. The thing to do with all uncomfortable feelings is to accept them. By accepting that we are uncomfortable with silence, we're being honest about our condition. We live in a society where we are constantly stimulated. Cities weren't designed to enable us to relax and reflect. Capitalism is not a system where wellbeing or relaxation matters. Constant economic growth leaves no place for reflection. Where's the profit in contemplation?

And so we make our way from morning to night agitated like popcorn in a hot pan. The media we consume is programmed to keep us wired rather than soothed. Why are radio and TV presenters so excited all the time? Nobody talks like that in the real world. Social media is no different. Algorithms give preference to anger, so these places are angry, yet we tune into them looking for some kind of peace.

Jesus, wouldn't it just make you want to climb into a tree and live there?

When we're thrust into silence, in a car, or an empty room, or the awkward, interminable void of an elevator with another occupant, we begin to feel uncomfortable in our skin. These are wonderful experiences, even if they can feel awkward, because this is when we're hovering close to the truth. This is just how it is. This is your reality. Recognising that you don't react well to silence is how we embrace honesty. And being honest with ourselves, and honest about our many weird and wonderful idiosyncrasies, is how we get a grip.

Please don't feel bad about this, but we all lie to ourselves. We say we're fine when we're anything but. When you recognise you're lying to yourself, the trick is to explore rather than avoid. And when you explore, if you're lucky you'll come across your madness. We've all got that too. The way we self-sabotage, or invest so much energy in worrying about things that won't happen, or how we behave in public, on dance floors, in public transport. There's a thick streak of madness in the way we act with each other. It's not damning, it's just how it is. We're socially anxious animals. But if we want to get a grip, we've first got to admit this. We have to come clean with ourselves. This is the only way we grow. It's a type of confession, except you can do it at any time and it doesn't involve a musty oak booth and prayer recital. And as we come clean it's important that we handle ourselves with kindness. It's not your fault that you turn the radio on first thing in the morning and leave it playing until you go to bed at night. It's not your fault that you can't imagine walking anywhere alone without a podcast or music in your ears. And it's really not your fault that you're constantly scrolling your phone in the search for joy, but when you see a certain person appear on your feed you find yourself defeated and running for the chocolate. These are just coping mechanisms necessary for when you've become uncomfortable in your own skin.

I had a student once who used to go to pieces whenever she thought about her ex. Then she'd beat herself up about it. 'It's been so many years,' she'd say, 'but whenever I think about him, or whenever he pops up in my feed, I feel sad and then I get frustrated.'

'Next time this happens, just say "Oh poor, poor brain,"' I said. 'It's not its fault. It's just tender. If you want it to change, don't chastise it, love it more.'

So she started imagining her brain as this unfortunate, tortured character, and each time the recriminations started, she'd say, 'Oh poor, poor brain,' and slowly, because nothing happens fast in meditation, she began to love her tender brain. 'I might as well get to like myself,' she told me one day, 'because I'm all I'm ever going to have.'

Getting a grip means learning to be okay with yourself, and we're never more ourselves than when we're silent.

I spent a winter housesitting a boathouse on the edge of Lough Derg. The house was damp and cold. I had no TV, no wi-fi, and a data plan that didn't really cover streaming content. These were the perfect conditions for a good meditator, so of course I, a scrappy meditator at best, got away from the place at every opportunity. I'd go on big walks every day up into the Arra Mountains overlooking Lough Derg. The mountains were mostly empty save for retired men in Millet rain gear with cellophane-wrapped sandwiches, sitting on boulders next to the peaks, happy to be out walking but dying for a conversation.

One man told me about a baby goat that had followed him back to the car. He brought it home, raised it, gave it milk from a bottle and when the kid was fully grown he brought it back to the mountain and chased it away with a stick.

'I did it with sadness,' he told me.

He was sitting on a boulder with a pair of binoculars, staring across at Moylussa.

'I look out for him, you know,' he said.

We come equipped with resilience, wisdom and bottomless depths of caring. Spending time with just ourselves, with just our thoughts, gives us the time to get to know this side of ourselves.

I try to spend at least a month out of every year on retreat. During that time I'll meditate but I'll also help run the retreat centre, cooking mountains of lentils, grating carrots until my fingers are stained like a smoker's, washing meditation cushions that have absorbed more physical tension in a week than an average cushion would know in five lifetimes. Nearly all of this happens without talking. If you're meditating there's certainly none of that, and if you're working it's kept to just the necessary communication. People who haven't been on retreat will often say, 'I couldn't go that long without talking.' I always reply, 'It's not the no-talking that gets you, it's the silence.'

If you go to Glendalough and you walk out towards the miners' village, along the flattish road that follows the upper lake, you can see a small cave across the water where St Kevin made his monastery. St Kevin was a lover of silence. There's a legend that he was so driven – and so cruel, I guess – that he drowned a woman who came to seduce him. Yikes.

But I can't imagine what a woman would see in some scrawny, tree-hugging monk who lived out under the rain all year long, and had very few career options. One legend about Kevin that I do like to believe, however, is the story of the blackbird. It goes like this: one day Kevin was sitting in silence when a bird came along and built a nest in his open hand. This bird then waited two weeks for the eggs to hatch, while all the time Kevin didn't as much as flinch.

Getting a grip is not something that happens overnight, or even after meditating for a few weeks. It's a lifetime pursuit. There's so much to you. So many parts. So many untapped areas, shadows, blind spots. Our goal in life is to learn to recognise them all and accept them all and love them all. Even the birds know this.

Exercise: Silence

Silence is the most confronting part of meditation, but it's only by becoming comfortable with silence that we learn to get a grip. By becoming comfortable with silence we learn, very simply, to be comfortable with ourselves.

Perform a short audit on your own auditory tendencies. Many of us only get quiet when we go to bed, and then we wonder why it's so hard to sleep at night. Think of all the times when you're avoiding silence: commuting with your phone in your hand, at home in the evenings in front of the TV, on your lunch break chatting with colleagues. Not to say that any of these things are bad, but when they become coping mechanisms or distractions from the dread of being in silence, then we might have a problem.

How about conversation? Can you actually let someone speak without interrupting them? Or how about this for next-level skills – can you spend company with someone else and just enjoy silence?

Is there a way that you can sneak a little more quiet time into your life? How about a walk in the evening with no phone? Or how about engaging in silence half an hour before you go to bed so it's not such a shock to the system when you finally put your head on the pillow?

Silence can be very loud when we first tune into it, but if you get used to it, silence can become your true home.

This Is It

One day at a time, sweet Jesus. Whoever wrote that one hadn't a clue. A day is a fuckin' eternity.

— RODDY DOYLE

Fulfillment isn't found over the rainbow – it's found in the here and now. Today I define success by the fluidity with which I transcend emotional land mines and choose joy and gratitude instead.

— RUPAUL

My favourite Irish expression is 'this is it'. In context, it's the most beautiful combination of words. When someone says 'this is it' it means that they couldn't be happier. It's rare to find people who couldn't be happier. Most people are not happy at all, or are working towards some great happiness in the future. Whenever I hear the words 'this is it', I pay attention, because it means that someone, either in my company or within earshot, is happy right now. And you don't want to miss that. It means that somebody's finally got it.

I have an older sister. We didn't always get along. Sometimes we'd fight for days. She was bigger and stronger than me, so I was sneaky. Younger brothers always are. One time we went on a family trip to Aillwee Cave in County Clare. At some point during the tour, the tour guide brought us into the deepest part of the cave and turned off the lights so we could experience the stalagmites and stalactites in pure blackness. I'm sure it was phenomenal. The caves are some of the best preserved in Europe, a place where over 10,000 years ago great Irish bears would go to die. The caves feel like an underground temple, but what did I care about that when I was eight years old and bitter? I only cared about revenge, so I used the cover of darkness to kick my sister hard in the shins. She screamed, I scuttled away like some deep cave-dwelling, conscience-less crustacean. Kelly, if you're reading this, I'm sorry but, in fairness, when you're little the only warfare you have is guerrilla.

Our parents would often try and resolve our conflict by making us sit in the same room together until we made peace. I knew a man who lived on Inis Mór who used the same technique on his dogs, who didn't like each other. He put both collies on the one rope. If one wanted to sniff something, the other had to be patient. If one wanted to take a shit the other had to just wait and watch. The peace Kelly and I made was born of similar compromised circumstances rather than any actual desire to get along.

Managing to just be with yourself is similar to being forced to make peace with your sibling, only the reward is not that you get to eat Viennetta after dinner, but that you get to be happy. The key to happiness is recognising that yes, this is it. If you don't manage to get along with yourself, then good luck getting along with others. You're all you have to work with, and this moment is the only one you can have any control over – this is it. If you're careful you'll find this incredibly empowering, because everything you need is already there and the tools are already in your hands. You are your greatest project – this is it.

I have two distinct memories of hearing this expression growing up. Both woke me in the way that a biscuit tin dropping off a shelf onto a hard stone floor will wake you.

Once, a very long time ago, I was on holiday with a girlfriend. We were in our early twenties and we were both bartenders. We had a fairly fractious relationship, but as we'd both been raised in homes where our parents showed love by arguing, we thought this was normal. We thought we were doing it properly. 'Sure we fight, but we stay together, isn't that the point?'

It's funny how we grow up in houses where we hate our parents' relationships, only to move out and find partners with whom we can replicate those relationships. I've dated people who felt like family; we'd say things to each other like, 'It feels like I've known you for so much longer.' The penny only dropped when we had our first argument. We date what's familiar to us but not what's necessarily good for us. That's the way.

Anyway, after a long summer of working, and so many late nights and lost keys and stealing cigarettes from each other, we decided to head out west for a holiday. We rented a B & B in Belmullet, and she rented a car because I had no licence back then. A healthy person would have delighted in the fact that his girlfriend could drive and save him having to take half a dozen buses across the country, but not me. My mind was wild back then, and the untrained mind can be a very ugly mind. I resented her for being able to drive when I couldn't. 'Rust never sleeps' is something they tell you when you're in the market for a second-hand car. It's very true. You can fix all kinds of motor malfunctions, but if the body is being chewed apart by rust, not much can be done. Resentment never sleeps either. Eventually it will eat you too.

My girlfriend was in a great mood. She sang to herself as we drove across Mayo. So often we think about things in terms of scarcity. If someone is happy, then it means there's less happiness around for us. This is wrong. One happy person is just pointing the way for the other unhappy people. One happy person is saying, 'Seriously, I'm coming down with this shit, I'm literally drowning in happiness, won't you please help yourself?' But we're funny creatures, no funnier than when we're being triggered, and the happier she became the more resentment built up in me. Either the details have become hazy or I'm too embarrassed to write them, but I seem to remember arriving at the B & B and making some awful scene because the pressure in the shower wasn't great. She replied that all I ever did was complain, which was 100 per cent accurate but not what I wanted to hear.

We got in the car and drove towards the sea. We had planned to walk around Erris Head, and if that meant taking the bristling tension with us, so be it. It was a beautiful dry evening. We followed a trail that cut close to the edge of the cliffs. There were seals in the water. A flock of sheep followed us for a spell, small-talking about this and that. There was a full moon hanging low over the water in a perfectly blue sky. It was one of those painfully beautiful evenings where Irish people born on the east of the country recognise that our island is a two-person horse costume and they've got the ass.

I walked behind my girlfriend, at a distance that symbolised we were together but unhappily so. We passed other walkers out that evening. They wore a combination of hi-vis vests and rugby shirts and gladly surrendered the path to us, rather than brush against our contagious mood. The sun began to set. And my girlfriend turned to me, and with no introduction, said the three small words: 'This is it.'

She was totally right. She had understood and articulated the present moment with the accuracy of a scientist. Buddha said there are three things you can't hide: the sun, the moon and the truth.

Despite myself, I smiled. The veil of mud lifted for a fraction. It was like someone making a joke in a prison yard, or a fart on an operating table. It was a dramatic intervention by the present. And although we didn't even last until August, that memory stuck.

You know we can do this? This is one of our superpowers. We can make a choice to drop our story any time. Try it for yourself. If you've got a story in your mind right now, just drop it as you might drop a glass from your hand.

I worked for a brief period as a war reporter in Afghanistan. It was an exciting and horrible job. Editors back in New York or London would phone you at four in the morning to tell you that a car bomb had exploded here, or a skirmish had erupted there, and could you get some footage before they went live with that morning's post? Every time you stepped outside your home to get a Coke from the local vendor, you had to ask yourself, do I want this Coke so badly that I'd risk getting kidnapped? Nine times out of ten, you did.

A photographer and I had been trying to get embedded with an American fighting unit in Kandahar. It would mean spending a few days side by side with a group of soldiers documenting the war. They'd try to keep me out of trouble but they couldn't guarantee it. I wouldn't want to do anything like that now, but back then I was young and had so much to prove. Knowing that my family and friends back in Europe were worried about me made me feel special. Does that sound familiar? I think a lot of young men engage in high-risk behaviour so they can feel special.

Before they'd let me join, they wanted to get to know me, so I visited the United States base in Kabul. It was a confusing time for the US military. Most of them had gone to Afghanistan with the belief that they were fighting a just war to liberate the Afghans from the Taliban. They couldn't understand why the Afghans hated them. Every time they tried to train locals to work with them they'd sit through the two-, three-day training programme, get kitted out in boots, combat gear and a gun, only to sneak away in the night and re-join the Taliban. Morale was low among the Americans. In conversation they compared war zones like other people compare restaurants. 'It's no Iraq, but it's a damn sight better than Somalia.'

Many sandbag walls and security checks later I was brought to a hospital wing in the middle of the base. The marine who took me there turned and said, 'When we saw on your application that you were Irish, we had to bring you to meet Captain Holohan.'

He brought me into a small ward where Captain Holohan was sitting in a wheelchair drinking a can of Red Bull with a straw. His face was covered in scratches. His arms too. His legs, from about the knee down, were nowhere to be seen.

'Are you the Irish guy?'

'I am.'

'Where you from?'

'Kildare.'

'Never heard of it,' he said. 'My parents are from Galway – Oughterard. Do you know it?'

'I know it well,' I said.

'Is it nice out there?'

'It's breathtaking.'

He lit up when I told him that, and then asked if I'd accompany him for a smoke. I followed him through the corridors out into a small courtyard with one palm tree in the middle that looked like it had been blasted with cement. On the open side of the courtyard was a wall of sandbags, topped with razor wire. Someone had painted the words 'Make-Out Point' across the sandbags. We both lit cigarettes and he pointed ahead of him. He didn't have an Irish accent but briefly he tried. He pointed out at the wall and the hazy sky above it, hazy because the air in Kabul was a mixture of dust, fumes and faecal matter, and the wiring that swung in great handfuls between buildings, and said, 'Sure, this is it.'

In the end I never got to do an embed with the Marines, and that was maybe for the best. I saw a suicide bombing one morning in Kabul and that was enough to keep me awake for half a year. I can't imagine what I might have had to endure if I'd been with an active combat unit.

Meditation has just one goal: to recognise that this is it. You're not trying to get anywhere, or change or improve anything. All your effort is pointed at the recognition of the present moment. We're meditating for the sake of meditating, and not for anything else. In meditation there is no goal. Every single state we enter is exactly the state we're meant to be in. If the mind is all stirred up, that's fine. If it's calm as a pond, that's also fine.

When I think of the expression 'this is it', I remember that it's never dependent on circumstances. You might be drinking tea out of a thermos in a tent beneath a torrent of rain, or lying in a poop-scattered pebble garden on a Sunday, or sitting in an open car boot eating a cheddar sandwich in a motorway service station in Offaly while the love of your life attempts in clichéd phrases and exasperated groans to explain to you what 'being triggered' means. It doesn't matter. It honestly doesn't matter.

What matters is being able to come to a place of acceptance of what is happening in the moment, and understand that you can neither change it, nor would you want to change it. This is it.

Exercise: This is it

We tend to reserve the expression 'this is it' for moments of deep relaxation and contentment, but if you use it at all times, it can act as a powerful reminder of what's really happening.

At no time can you say 'this is it' and find that it's not true.

Every single moment that passes, you get to choose whether you really dive into the experience of it, or if you want to distract yourself.

By remembering 'this is it' in uncomfortable times and 'this is it' during comfortable times, your life can become a lot like meditation.

For a while I changed the lock screen on my phone to the words 'this is it'. It cut my phone usage down a lot, not as much as I'd have liked, but still.

You could write it on your hand. Or maybe on a Post-it that you stick on your mirror. A face tattoo even?

By remembering this regularly you can learn that there's no goal to life. You're not trying to get anywhere or become anything, you're just trying to recognise that this, and this alone, is it.

How to Be Happy Out

When anyone asks me about the Irish character,
I say look at the trees. Maimed, stark and mis-
shapen, but ferociously tenacious.

— EDNA O'BRIEN

There is great happiness in not wanting, in not
being something, in not going somewhere.

— JIDDU KRISHNAMURTI

My great-granddad Jack was an orphan. He never knew his
parents and was raised in a state institution in Portlaoise.
He went on to marry, become a bar owner and have four
children, twelve grandchildren and thirty-something
great-grandchildren who adored him like a Disney toy. I
don't know much about the early details of his life, but we
all know that babies need to be held, and gazed at and sung
to, or else their play-dough bodies don't develop properly.
We know that babies need to be told they're safe, lovable,
pretty and smart or they never get those ideas themselves.
My great-grandfather would have got none of this at the
orphanage. At best, he got picked up once or twice a day.
Of all the godforsaken places in all the godforsaken world,

he came to live as an orphan in post-famine Ireland. We never spoke about karma, me and Jack. To be honest, we didn't talk much, considering I was still getting the hang of words, and steps and balance, but if we had, if I could have convinced him to indulge his great-grandchild in a little Eastern superstition, then maybe we would have had a conversation about karma.

Karma simply means that your struggles in the present are connected to problems from your past. That could mean past lives, if you're so inclined to believe in reincarnation, or simply your childhood, or your youth, or what you did last summer. You don't have to believe in reincarnation to meditate, but there's no guarantee that you won't by the end. There are lots of things you may or may not believe in by the end – you, reality, time, they'll all be up for debate after a while.

One of the first teachers I met when I went to India was a man called Dr Jivasu. He had trained as a paediatrician in Canada but was now based in Rishikesh. The Beatles went to Rishikesh. It's considered one of India's holiest places but it's also a bit like Burning Man Festival. If you're truly spiritual you probably don't wind up in Rishikesh, you travel further into India, but even trees start off small, and this is where new seekers often start their search.

Every evening Dr Jivasu would give a talk by the River Ganges that was attended by about a hundred people. After the talk, people would stay behind and ask him questions, and sometimes he wouldn't get out of the building until long after midnight. That didn't bother him; he admitted to only sleeping four hours a night anyway. One time, I asked him a question. 'Dr Jivasu, what's the one thing that can help a meditation practice?'

'Struggle,' he said. 'The more you have in your life, the more you'll seek an end to it. It's actually good karma to be born with a struggle. Struggle will ignite your journey. Go find your struggle and at the end of your struggle, you'll find happiness.'

Of all the people I've met, and I've been blessed to have met some great desert monks who lived off less than a handful of rice a day, and Himalayan babas who had spent entire decades living in caves, and shamans who could close their eyes and inhabit the bodies of crows and fly to the next pueblo to tell you if your bus was on time – or so they claimed – I never met a happier human than my great-granddad. He made something magical of his life. I could see that when I wasn't even potty trained.

There's a saying that babies and those near the end of their life are closest to the gods. And those in the middle of their life, the ones with mortgages and young families, are furthest away. And so it was, while the grown-ups were busy running around and trying to get a handle on life, they'd drop me off at Jack's. At this stage he was in his nineties and I was a toddler. We walked at about the same pace. We'd take the dogs out along the canal, and if the dogs decided to find a patch of grass to lie down in, we'd do the same.

'Lovely,' he'd say. 'This is just lovely.'

That was his catchword. He had an uncanny way of always finding something beautiful worthy of your attention. He knew the names of some of the trees, but it didn't stop him giving names to the ones he didn't know. 'The big dark one', 'the curly one', 'the half-broke gamey one'.

In spring, we'd plant potatoes and I'd be his assistant, following after him as he ploughed the earth with an old wooden hoe. He'd laugh when I dropped the potatoes in root upwards instead of down. 'Maybe you've invented a new way of farming,' he'd say.

Unlike Jack, my great-grandmother was an axe. She could shoot a gun and drive a car, and was held in such reverence and fear that, on her very last hospital visit, before she finally died, the nurses allowed her to smoke a Silk Cut out the window of her room. Just to put it in context, this was the nineties, not post-war Ireland. She passed shortly afterwards, aged ninety-six. She wasn't the most loving woman. Or at least she didn't show her love in a way that you could readily understand. This is something I've learned: many people do love you but don't know how to show it. I think this was the case with my great-grandmother. I can't remember ever sitting on her lap, and when I think of her face now, when I think how it looked close up, all I can remember is long yellow teeth and a thick Kildare accent that sounded archaic or remote, or from some kind of parallel Kildare that had yet to be electrified, yet to be awakened to the linguistic fluency of RTÉ.

She grumbled. There was a little bitterness in her. Maybe it came from living next to the happiest man on the planet, yet never learning the secrets of his happiness. Jack just smiled when she snapped at him, and then loved her a little more, which, I'm guessing from my own experience in relationships where there's an imbalance of happiness, probably just made her angrier.

Buddha told a story once. He was travelling through India teaching people how to meditate, and in one village he passed through a local holy man became so angry that Buddha's popularity had depleted his followers that he decided to go find him and attack him. At the time,

Buddha was under a tree giving a talk. Buddha saw the man approaching from afar. Buddha could tell that the guy was angry, not because Buddha had special powers – even though he did – but because the guy was fuming and ranting as he stormed up the field to the tree where Buddha was sitting.

Buddha wasn't afraid. He shouted out to him: 'Can I ask you one question?'

'Yes,' the man replied, 'but it will be the last question you ever ask.'

'What do you do if someone comes to your house with a gift that you don't want?'

'What a stupid question. You tell them to keep the gift and take it with them.'

'Well then, you can keep your anger and you can take it with you. I don't want it. Thank you.'

Until he could no longer support the weight of his own body, Jack would make my great-grandmother porridge every morning and bring it to her in bed. Sometimes I think of those first few cold mornings after he'd gone. How was it to wake up and not hear him opening drawers, catch the smell of the gas burning, the sound of his slippers shuffling across the linoleum floor and the dogs beating their tails against his legs, and him telling them to calm down and his soft voice only making them more excited? Dogs loved him even more than his family did. I used to think about my great-grandmother waking up and reaching across for the hotspot on the mattress. After seventy-five years of breakfast in bed, had she forgotten how to feed herself?

If I had to distil it into a formula – if I had to develop a recipe for how Jack moved through life without the anguish, the stickiness, the neurosis that characterise most of our movements – it was his ability to just not let anything bother him. He could just let anything go. Nothing stuck to my great-granddad. Not bad weather, bad moods or bad luck.

Jack Kornfield, the meditation teacher and my great-granddad's namesake, has this beautiful quote.

> In the end
> these things matter most:
> How well did you love?
> How fully did you live?
> How deeply did you let go?

My great-granddad was such a master at loving, living and letting go because he'd begun with so little, because he'd grown up with so much suffering. He'd grown up with such a strong need for love that was never satisfied. There's a lot to be said for suffering. In Buddhism, your very first task is to recognise that all life is in fact suffering. This is often the point where people part ways with Buddhism, though. They think, 'Shit, suffering? I came here for an end to that, not more of it.'

Duhka is the term Buddhists use for this. It's very simple and, despite what folks think, very positive. *Duhka* means that everything outside yourself, everything in life, has a tinge of dissatisfaction to it. The satisfaction gained from things, objects and feelings don't last. The work-around for this is just to recognise it, and know that your true happiness, the thing deep inside you, cannot be annihilated. So next time you find yourself heartbroken, miserable or tearing up a lottery ticket and throwing it into the wind, go back to that place if you can. It never disappoints.

The clearest way to recognise suffering is on retreat. When I go on retreat, high in the mountains or tucked away in the countryside, we'll sit in rows with our legs crossed on the floor of some cold assembly room for the guts of fourteen hours a day. There's no talking, no reading material. There's plenty of food, except you only get to eat during a tiny window at the start of the day. Retreats are designed to give you deeper insights into the nature of life, but you can only get these insights if you suffer a little, and then when you recognise you're suffering, you learn to let go.

That's how it is, you're sitting there on the cushion and you're trying to meditate, and before you know it, because your mind doesn't give a shit that you're on retreat, you're flooded with thoughts. You think about sex, you think about food, you think about all the things you want to do in this lifetime, and then immediately you begin to suffer because you're on retreat, you've signed up to join a type of silent prison where there's certainly no sex, there's barely anything to eat and you're offline for the next ten days, so good luck launching the business idea that came to you at five o'clock this morning. The suffering starts because you want and you can't have, or you don't want but you have. The suffering starts because the reality we've been presented with is unappealing to us, and we think that because we really are very exceptional people, this is terribly unfair.

Jack had a great sense of what was fair. He knew that some babies got born into loving families, and others in institutions. This equipped him with superhuman capabilities of perspective from the earliest age. He'd used his struggle to grow wise. He was compassionate because he knew what it was like to suffer. He was loving because he knew how valuable love is. And he was grateful, making sure to announce each bit of goodness he encountered in the same way people announce full moons and rainbows – 'This is just lovely!'

One time, we were eating ice cream in the back garden. Inside there was a football semi-final playing on the TV. The rest of my older cousins were watching it and shouting at the screen. I was older now, so Jack must have been very close to the end. It was only months away. Maybe even his last summer.

'Why don't you watch the football?' I asked him.

'Oh that, too much excitement,' he said. 'I'm happy out here.'

Exercise: Gratitude

If you're not born with preternatural happiness skills, you can work on it. The best way is to increase your capacity for gratitude. Gratitude is like a muscle. It can be trained, toned and made stronger. We train it by doing reps. Every day, you choose three unique things that you're grateful for. You can do this at any time of the day. I like to hook it on to when I'm cleaning my teeth.

At the beginning it's easy: I'm grateful for the sun, I'm grateful for coffee, I'm grateful for my home, my dog, that my phone is fully charged. But by as early as day four or five, it can get hard for some people. In the same way that when we began to meditate we realised our mind was out of control, when we begin to exercise our gratitude muscle, we realise, oh man, it's really, really weak.

That's why we exercise it every day. You've got to get those reps in.

Over time, practising gratitude changes your entire outlook on life.

You miss the bus to work, yet you turn it into a positive because you're grateful that another bus is on the way in five minutes.

You get rained on on the way home but you feel gratitude that you have an umbrella, and you have a home and don't need to sleep outdoors.

You miss out on a job opportunity but you're grateful that you were considered in the first place, and you see that, yes this is tough, but it's also progress.

Does this feel like a bit of a stretch? Like, seriously, this guy expects me to be grateful when I just got turned down for a job?

Just try it yourself. I've met some Olympic-level gratitude-practisers who've broken their legs and could still find reasons to be cheerful that they hadn't broken their arms too. I had a student arrive late to a workshop because his bike was stolen. Everyone in the room felt bad for him, but he didn't feel bad for himself.

'It's cool,' he said. 'I'd had it for three years and it served me well that whole time. I'm feeling very lucky that I've had a bike so long, to be honest.'

Gratitude is the gateway to optimism, because gratitude equips you with resilience:

- You fall ill, but instead of thinking you've been singled out for unfair treatment, you imagine all the people in the world who are in a worse state than you.
- You go to the fridge and your housemate's finished all the oat milk, so you have to take your coffee black, but you're grateful just the same because, let's be honest, coffee is life, with or without the hipster bainne.

Mindfulness vs Balubas

I didn't feel with her, like I did with many other people, that while I was talking she was just preparing the next thing she wanted to say.

— SALLY ROONEY

The ultimate source of all problems is in thought itself, the very thing of which our civilization is most proud, and therefore the one thing that is 'hidden' because of our failure seriously to engage with its actual working in our own individual lives and in the life of society.

— DAVID BOHM

One of my favourite poems is Portia Nelson's 'Auto-biography in Five Short Chapters'. The chapters are so short they're actually just a few sentences. It's not a real autobiography at all. It's purely figurative. This is Portia Nelson's clever joke and why poets are special people and why we need them.

In each chapter of the poem the poet walks down a street. In the first few chapters she falls into the same hole each time. The protagonist transforms from being surprised by this to expecting it to happen. In the second-last chapter, she finally walks around the hole. In the last chapter – chapter five – she walks down another street, a street where there are no holes. The message from the poem is simple: you can't rely on your city council to finish the jobs they start, and the only way to prevent yourself from self-inflicted harm is knowing what you're doing.

Welcome to mindfulness.

Everyone uses the word 'mindful' these days. I was in transit through Atlanta airport some years back when a woman from border security stopped me to say, 'Sir, be mindful of your shoelaces.' They were undone. I thanked her.

Once upon a time I was out rock climbing with a friend in Clare. It was our first time climbing together, and understandably he had some trust issues. He tied in his rope and was about to make his first moves up the wall when he turned to me and said, 'You will be mindful of the rope, won't you?'

'I will,' I said, 'and I'll hold on to it too.'

Mindfulness, like 'going forward', 'circle back' and 'double-click', has become a part of our jargon. We tend to switch off or roll our eyes when we hear it. It can have the same effect as when someone says 'mind your manners', which is to say, the same effect as fingernails on a blackboard. This is a shame because mindfulness is very important. It's actually the heart of Buddhist meditation, and the key to navigating this great big shitshow we call life.

I think many people confuse mindfulness with being happy or being blissed out. This is untrue – but, more than untrue, it's actually really unfair. You can be broken-hearted and mindful. You can be angry and mindful. You can be resentful, small and bitter, and still mindful. You can be lonely as fuck and still be mindful. You can be at rock bottom and mindful. Mindfulness is not a silver bullet, it's just seeing things as they really are.

We have a slogan in this meditation world: Feel more, hurt less. That means more sadness, more anger, more love, more loss and maybe, very occasionally, more bliss. It's the big picture unfolding in front of you without your usual crutches and distractions. It's confronting. Mindfulness means exposing yourself completely to who you are. This requires huge courage.

So if someone tells you that mindfulness leaves them feeling perpetually blissed out without a care in the world, they might just be having you on.

One of my favourite recent Irish books is Anna Burns's *Milkman*. Did you read it? In it she describes the 'dark mental energies' found in some Northern Irish communities. I know these communities well. They're my family. Every Christmas, every Easter, we'd make our way up to our relatives in Belfast and immerse ourselves in their doilies, their English TV, their red, white and blue painted kerbs and come home with money that the shopkeepers wouldn't accept, and new accents and phrases that took weeks to shake: 'Whataboutcha' instead of 'Howsitgoinhorse'. I always found these places harder than Kildare. The humour was rougher. In Kildare, I was occasionally called carrots; up there, every day, I was a wee ginger bastard.

My friends in Northern Ireland grew up faster than my friends in the South. They knew about drugs when we were just learning about alcohol. If we got into fist fights, they were already fighting with knives. One boy gave me a condom when I was only fourteen. 'You might get a dart while you're up here, Conor.' It stayed in my wallet for about two years and then ended up in a washing machine, and then in a bin. So long, promises of youth. I remember one time, out kicking a ball against the red, white and blue kerbs, seeing two young lads coax a small boxer pup closer to them only to throw stones at it.

There is a distinct and unmistakable energy difference between Northern Ireland and the Republic. Those dark mental energies. Victim complexes galore – 'I've been treated so bad, and that's why I treat others that way.' When I began to explore my own mind, I found that my

Northern Irish accent didn't last more than two weeks down south, but my own victim complex had taken roots that had lasted all my life.

When I first began becoming mindful of my own thoughts and habits, I recognised that my victim complex prevented me from seeing my privilege and empathising with others. I too had a head full of dark mental energies. Because of this, I hurt a lot of people in my twenties. I felt that I was more deserving than they were. When you've been treated unfairly, you can become a little blind. It can make it hard to believe that others have been treated unfairly too. We become so focused on our pain that we can't imagine anybody else feels it. As I began to observe this in myself, I could see it in my entire Northern Irish family.

My grandfather, who had been in the RAF, told my dad, 'Don't give them children of yours taig names.' We are Conor and Kelly and my dad was and always will be a shit-stirrer of the highest order. I think, despite our names, that my granddad learned to love us to the best of his abilities.

In the *vipassana* tradition of meditation where I cut my teeth, the teacher constantly repeats the slogan, 'The reality as it is, not how you want it to be.' You hear this so often that by the time you go home again, it seems to ring in your ears like shell shock. Whenever I hear this expression I think of my family up north. Peace requires empathy. Empathy requires mindfulness. Mindfulness means going deep beneath the stories we tell ourselves and facing who we really are. This is why, when it comes to understanding mindfulness, it can help to go right back to the source: Buddhism.

In Buddhism they call mindfulness *sati*. It means conscious awareness with an attitude of equanimity. Simply put, as you observe yourself and the world around you, you do so without deciding if something is good or bad, you just observe it as it is. When we're on autopilot, or let's call it mindlessness, you jump from one situation to the next making judgement after judgement. We're like some overly zealous bureaucrat with a rubber stamp, slapping pages in front of us: reject/pass.

Here is a snapshot of our thoughts at any time of the day: I don't like what he's wearing. I do like this coffee. I don't like this wind. I don't like her face. I hate that song. I want chocolate, no I actually want to pee. Do I really want to pee, or am I maybe just horny? Christ, I'm actually both.

Judging is a reflex. It's not so different from what happens when someone puts an open packet of biscuits beside you. This is such an Irish cliché as to be almost a ritual. You arrive in someone's home. They offer you tea, which you accept. And they offer you some biscuits, which you refuse, but they still take them out of the cupboard and place them in front of you anyway. Ten biscuits later, they've a huge grin on their face and you've a sugar high that'll rob you of half of your sleep. The same thing might happen with drink, or when someone wants you to go in on a bag of drugs with them.

We're helpless when we're mindless, and we're mindless almost all the time. Think about the last time you went to the fridge. Were you even hungry or maybe just a little bored? Or the times you text people: do you really want to talk, or are you just uncomfortable, agitated, seeking some drama to bring significance into your life?

We go through life being battered by impulses, and the most powerful impulse is judging. We can want to avoid, attack, ignore, devour and kiss all in the space of a minute. When we're mindful, we're waking up from this cycle. We're waking up and recognising that we're in a constant state of reaction to the world around us and this is what keeps us in this uncomfortable state of being – either hyper or depressed, but rarely at ease.

Kerry, our family dog, had so many skin conditions towards the end of her life that it was hard for her to lie down. She'd circle for what seemed like ten minutes before dropping, only to get up almost immediately and do it all over again. She was always uncomfortable and it was hard to watch. When we're reacting rather than just observing, this is how we go through life: like elderly Dalmatians with chronic bronzing syndrome.

With mindfulness we're finally understanding our own minds and seeing how the stories we tell ourselves are just that – stories. We don't have to believe them any more. Our stories are cages that we build for ourselves. Mindfulness is freedom. Being mindful means that you're awake – but there's no guarantee that the thing you're waking up to will be a meadow. Or a junkyard. When we're mindful we're learning to know ourselves completely, and this can mean uncovering parts of us that we don't like. We all have shadows. Unless, of course, you're a vampire.

My grandparents from Belfast only came south long after my parents were married and my sister and I – our taig names unaltered – were no longer babies. They'd been scared to cross the border before that. They'd been scared of Catholics. I remember they always brought packed lunches with them and supplies of tinned meats and bread. My grandmother carried Dettol disinfectant in her handbag, like a backpacker travelling through a dengue zone in India or South America. But despite their fear and resistance, they fell in love with the South. It got to the point where they'd take their holidays without us. They'd just drive straight on through Kildare until they hit west Cork and Owenahincha beach.

When my grandmother was in a nursing home towards the end of her life, I'd call her on the phone every now and then. She wasn't always the warmest of people, but she wanted to be warm. You had to coax the warmth out of her with kindness: 'I love you, Ella'; 'I love you too, Conor.' She enjoyed it eventually, but it was sometimes like convincing a feral cat to come out from under the house and take the milk. She told me she hadn't expected what she found when she crossed the border.

'What did you find, Ella?'

'Everyone was friendly and they didn't care where we were from.'

When she died, I asked for her blanket. It was a striped woollen thing with tassels. She wrapped it around her legs every day when she was in the home. It went in the boot of my car and has now been at Fusion Festival, Electric Picnic, Melt, a few rainbow gatherings, an anarchist squat in Warsaw and a nudist beach in Croatia. It's seen more of the world than my grandmother could ever have dreamed.

Exercise: Mindfulness

Set a timer on your phone for one minute.

Sit down.

Begin to become aware of the breath in your nose, or your chest or your stomach.

Close your eyes and as thoughts appear, just remember to bring your awareness back to your breathing.

From this perspective, connected to the breath, you'll notice that you can observe your thoughts rather than think your thoughts.

Keep doing this for one-minute intervals, whenever you want.

Graduate to doing it with your eyes open.

Keep training your ability to observe thoughts rather than think thoughts.

As you go through your day, become aware of the thoughts that are influencing you and see if you can observe them rather than respond to them.

When they say jump, can you say why?

Observing your thoughts is the pathway to waking up, and waking up is freedom.

If It's Under a Rock, You'll Find It

I remember, as a child, a particular groan that my father would sound when he crawled from the bed in the morning. I hear the same groan now, precisely, every morning, when I emerge from my own lair. It's more than an expression of physical weariness – it's an aching of the soul. Even the groans get passed down.

— KEVIN BARRY

Life's work is to wake up.

— PEMA CHÖDRÖN

I never set out to write a meditation memoir. All I wanted to do was write a book about meditation that was slightly more palatable to an Irish audience than the books you normally find in self-help/spiritual/esoteric/miscellaneous sections in bookshops.

Not that I have anything against those books, but I always found them kind of embarrassing. If I was in Waterstones and somehow found myself browsing in that section, I'd pray that I wouldn't run into anyone I knew. Meditation books just looked so lame to me. They were uniformly designed with sky-blue covers, landscape stock photographs of valleys or sunsets and titles that looked like B & B bathroom wisdom: 'If you sprinkle when you tinkle, be a sweetie and wipe the seatie.'

It was like they were written for children. I felt they were patronising me. Tara Brach, Jack Kornfield, Sharon Salzberg, and even Eckhart Tolle, with his half-speed speech and his woollen waistcoats, made me angry. I revere these people now like teenagers revere rock stars, but at one stage they got under my skin.

This is useful: the people who get under your skin are pointing you towards the parts of your self that need healing. There are many stumbling blocks on the way to finding peace, but the biggest one is always going to be yourself.

The last people to try meditation are the cynics, and I know this because I am one. Even today, many years after taking the red pill, I'm still a little cynical. I find it hard to say '*namaste*', for example, and the only time you'll catch me making prayer hands is in an emoji, or under peer pressure. There's a resistance in me that's maybe in many Irish people. God, we have had so much religion that anything that even smells like it can make us feel queasy.

Another aspect is authenticity. The meditation world is full of frauds. Not like second-hand car dealer frauds, just folks who haven't done enough personal work to recognise that their intentions are not good.

Being a meditation teacher is an ego trap. I should know – I went off to write a simple meditation book only to make it all about *moi*! In fairness, and in hindsight, I think I wanted to write a book for myself, or at least my former self, the one who would have sneered at the idea of reading a spiritual book. He might have had an aneurysm on the spot, if I'd told him one day he'd actually write one.

Still, cynical as I was, I can still remember flirting with spirituality, and I did come close to the shore even if I didn't land. If you're a cynic and you're reading this, then let me warn you, you're also coming close to the shore. Any closer and you might have to land.

When I was fifteen, my parents allowed me to go to Dublin on my own for the first time. If you grew up in Dublin, I feel sorry for you, because you will never quite understand the thrill that a culchie experiences on arrival there. Excitement, when it's real, is a cocktail that includes a dash of fear. That was Dublin for me as a teenage bogger. From the minute the bus turned onto the quays and the Guinness stacks came into view, your heart would begin to beat faster and you'd move your wallet from a back pocket – country style – to a front one, because you knew that while Dublin was a place of great wonder and excitement, it was also home to drug addicts, pickpockets, lock-hards and head-the-balls who could identify sweet country folk by their gait. This was once explained to me by a man on Inis Oírr. His name was Paraic Pol. He was a wild man with sideburns and straw hair and a geansaí made of wool that looked like the sheep hadn't fully relinquished it yet.

He hated Dublin. He said it was unnatural. 'There's actual shite in the air,' he said, 'actual faecal matter borne by the wind.' He told me how, whenever he had to go there for some bureaucratic reason or other, he would modify his walk. What he told me about walking stuck.

'Island people and country people in general, we have a walk to us,' he said. 'We raise our feet higher on account of the ground beneath us always being precarious. A natural Dubliner never has to consider balance or that the ground might go from under him, or that a puddle as deep as your knee that wasn't there yesterday might have opened up overnight. As soon as I come out of Busáras, I start walking with my feet closer to the ground, and they never spot it.'

Temple Bar was the equivalent of Haight-Ashbury for me back then. I'd hang around on the edge of the Dublin teenagers, my head hidden by a poncho that I'd bought at Eager Beaver, and listen out for their slang words so I could learn to speak like them. They didn't shift, they met. They didn't say feen, they said man. Good things weren't munya, they were sweet.

My teenage years were coated in a thick film of crippling social anxiety. I had been a bright, open child, but I changed into a pimply gargoyle of a lad who spoke in mutters and sighs. I didn't make many friends, but there were people who would talk to you in Temple Bar without you making the first move: the Hare Krishnas. I was constantly returning home with free spiritual books. I had enough copies of the Bhagavad Gita to build a book wall with, yet I never read the thing. Still, I was drawn to the idea of peace and solitude, even if I didn't like the Hare Krishnas so much, and could never get into their books.

One day a Hare Krishna called Brendan, from Gort originally, sat down beside me. He stank, not of dirt and sweat, but of patchouli oil, wholewheat bread, turmeric, charcoal toothpaste and mossy deodorants. He wasn't dressed up like the rest of them. He was in shorts and a jumper. 'Wearing shorts in winter is a sign of how spirituality advanced you are,' a friend from east Clare told me once when we saw a guy wearing Reef sandals on a frosty morning as we went to buy bread in Aldi. Brendan, the trainee Hare Krishna from Gort, dressed the same.

'You know you don't have to be a Hare Krishna to be happy,' he said.

'Why do you do it, then?'

'It's my family,' he said. 'It's not for everyone.'

'It's really not for me.'

'Fair enough. Do you meditate?'

'What's that?'

'Just look at your breath. Look at it as it comes in, and look at it as it goes out. That's it. That's how you wake up.'

'You sound like you're talking to a child with learning difficulties, Brendan.'

'Well if a child can't understand it, how's an adult supposed to?'

I was very guarded when I was younger. Waking up, in the spiritual sense, means letting that guard down. It doesn't mean that you become gullible, but you learn to trust in your own instinct, rather than becoming bogged down with your own logic, your own patterns, and all the different voices you've picked up along the way.

We don't make things easy for ourselves when it comes to making decisions. There is an easier way for us to navigate our way through life, but we rarely take it. In general, when presented with two or more options, we don't come to our conclusion by relying on our intuition; we follow an agonising process of self-doubt, fear-based rationalisations and epic battles within ourselves that leave us exhausted. If you're reading this and you're tired, there's a good chance that you're resisting something in yourself.

Waking up simply means nourishing what we've always known to be true. I spent the majority of my life running away from what I knew to be true. It took me nearly twenty years to meditate again after that first day, when Brendan the Hare Krishna showed me how. But this is just the process. These things take time. Stop for a second, and see if you can feel something inside you, maybe a voice or a sensation, then try to pay a little more attention to that. Put the book on your lap and just try for a minute. This is your instinct. Of all the many situations and people you'll meet in this world, all the bosses, the lovers, the tribes you bond with, nobody will have your best interest at heart quite like your own instinct.

My grandmother has met quite a few of my girlfriends over the years. I know she'd love me to be settled, to have kids of my own, to bring them to meet her so she could bounce them on her knee, smell their unique scent. But she also recognises that this might not happen in her lifetime. We've spoken about it. Whenever she's asked me, 'How's such and such?', and I've answered, 'Oh, we're no longer together,' she doesn't judge. Instead she says, 'Don't worry, my dear, if she's under a rock you'll find her.'

Waking up could be subtitled 'If it's under a rock you'll find it.' It's a process of distillation. By annihilating all the other options you eventually arrive at the one thing that is true. Once you've untangled all the negative voices and the habit patterns that you pick up and adopt as you proceed through life, you come to a place where you find the real you. The real you is basically just the most authentic possible version of you. It's the one who's been waiting to emerge all this time, only you were possibly too scared to let them out.

A teacher in India once told me that if you're drawn towards meditation and solitude, you were probably a monk in another life. This might make you cringe. People in India – okay, let me rephrase, tourists in India are always coming out with unsubstantiated things like this. It suits the reassuring narrative that everything is planned neatly and perfectly, that if it's under a rock you'll find it.

But if you're reading this book right now, you must know something's up. I did too, only my story is less glamorous than some Indian hill-top baptism of insight. I'd have to attribute my coming to meditation to the persuasive power of Facebook's advertising algorithms. An algorithm so smart, so kind, so divine really, that it could tell by my hours of scrolling and scrolling that what I needed was not an advert for cheap fashion or collapsible furniture but a subscription to a mindfulness app. It began with the seeds planted by Hare Krishnas on wet summer afternoons in Temple Bar, but it really grew with a Facebook free trial for Headspace.

Exercise: Tuning into your instinct

If you watch your thoughts you'll notice that between each one is a space. You can call this the space between. The space between can be a little like sunlight on a cloudy day. It's not always easy to locate. But by becoming aware of the space between your thoughts, you're beginning to shed light on the most important part of you: your instinct.

In spiritual parlance we call this 'the one who knows'. Your thoughts are a storm of future-based speculations, past regrets and fear of the unknown, but the space between is a place where you are not contending with problems, where you are entirely present and where you know what you need. The way to spend more time in the space between, rather than in, thoughts is to recognise it. It's like the Tinkerbell effect – believe it and you'll see it.

Look away from the page for a short while and just become aware of the thoughts that are passing through your head right now. And they are passing. If you look at them rather than think them, that's how they behave. And while you're looking, watch out for when they tail off, and for a second, maybe less, maybe more, you'll find yourself looking at the space between.

That's also where you'll find all the answers you need.

The Fear

Being Irish, he had an abiding sense of tragedy, which sustained him through temporary periods of joy.

— WB YEATS

Fear is a natural reaction to moving closer to the truth.

— PEMA CHÖDRÖN

A healthy relationship with fear is necessary if you want to walk the spiritual path, because the path is littered with challenges, obstacles and the occasional dog poop.

First let me establish a distinction. There's the fear we experience when we're in real danger and then the fear we experience when we recognise that the rug beneath our feet is about to get pulled away. This is the fear we need to embrace. It's the fear of losing control. It's the fear of an adventure. It's the fear that something big, some great love, some great move, some exploration or some personal growth is about to happen.

I once heard this story from a teacher in California. She looked a lot like Storm from the X-Men. You'll find that many meditation teachers have an unearthly quality to them, that is until they need a place to stay when they're in town, and then you realise that they forget to put their mugs in the sink just like everyone else. 'Life,' she said, 'is like getting into a small boat with an oar that you can't always locate, and heading along a giant river that you've never navigated before but you know ends at some stage in a treacherous waterfall that'll smash your boat to pieces and kill you instantly.'

Gulp.

'If this was a ride at a fun park,' she said, 'nobody would sign up for it, but somehow here we all are. How's the water in your part of the river?'

'Choppy, to be honest.'

The fear that we experience in meditation is often meeting the parts of us that we've tried to paper over or suppress. If you haven't spent much time with your mind it can be a lot like a bad neighbourhood with certain parts that you'd never venture into at night, and certainly not alone. Many of us spend our whole lives trying to avoid these parts of us. I get it. I have these mental neighbourhoods too. They're scary.

Being busy is a great way of avoiding getting to know yourself.

'Mr Duffy ... lived at a little distance from his body,' writes Joyce in *Dubliners*. Don't we all at different stages? How often have you been sick, or in pain, or upset, but managed to occupy yourself so completely that you didn't notice? Here's a simple rule of thumb: the busier you are, the less you enjoy being with yourself.

My mother asked my granddad on his deathbed if he had any regrets. He was heavily sedated at the time, but he could still get some words out. 'I wish I'd played more music,' he said, 'and not run a bar.' My granddad had been a jazz musician until he was forced to take over his dad's bar. He never liked it. He was a star; he didn't enjoy a life of service, sweeping up, dealing with drunks, picking up their dropped change, spilled pints, piss all over the walls. I inherited bartending from my granddad, and for the most part I inherited his dislike of it too. My granddad was sad. He only had the nerve to admit it right at the end, on his deathbed, because any sooner would have broken him in two.

For many of us, the thing we're afraid of looking at is the deep pool of sadness at our core. We're afraid that if we so much as glance at it, the walls might collapse and the sadness drench us. But you can't run away from your sadness for ever. Eventually, you'll have to sit down and talk to it.

This is why when we do sit down, on our own, and with our minds, it's an act of immense courage. By simply sitting with our thoughts, rather than feeding the inclination to escape them though distractions, we are staring down the monsters who torment us and saying, 'I see you. Go on, break my heart, I can take it.'

Between the ages of about eighteen and twenty-one, I worked in a nightclub in Dublin called the Kitchen, which was owned by U2. It was the very late nineties, a sweet moment in Dublin's history. In some ways the city felt fairer, even if the ground-breaking legislation that swept through with the two referendums hadn't happened yet. It was so much more affordable. A bartender or a waitress could afford to live in a modern apartment that, fair enough, might be a bit damp, and sure the balcony might just get used for storing bins until collection day, but it still felt metropolitan and continental even if most days the wind might cut your head off if you stepped out onto it.

All my friends at the time lived in these kinds of places. All of us knew too much about drugs. And all of us spent our weekends partying, which meant that all of us were deeply acquainted with something we called 'the fear'. The fear is when you wake up from a night out with an unshakeable belief that you've done something really bad the night before. For many people, and for me for many years, it was a feature of most weekends. The fear can range from just being scared that you let some secret out of the bag, or perhaps that you got into an argument with someone or maybe that you drunk-texted an ex or, worse, you shifted one.

This feeling lifted by the late afternoon or early evening when you realised that you'd not received any angry text messages yet, and that everyone else was drunk so no doubt they were feeling the same fear, and if you had done something anyone there wouldn't remember anything about the night anyway. If you took drugs the fear was the same beast, albeit with sabre-tooth fangs, retractable claws and advanced training in psychological torture. This fear kicked in with a slight delay, arriving the day after the day after, when the serotonin levels in your body had returned to normal and you were visited by damning thoughts about your choices, your direction, your place in this wild arena called life.

The fear is an Irish export. I've met Australians and Germans who talk about it because they partied with Irish people. In other places, in cultures where they're not so uncomfortable talking about their mental health, they just call fear what it really is: anxiety. Anxiety is very normal.

We all have it to some degree or another. You don't get to live in this world, have a job, commute to work, date, own a phone without it. But we don't talk about it openly enough; instead we wrap it up in comical ghoulish language and call it 'the fear'. Why is it so hard to be honest about our anxiety, when it's as much a part of modern life as air pollution? Perhaps naming it 'anxiety' means that we have to take it seriously. 'The fear', less so.

Everyone in our group respected the fear. For example it was generally fine to excuse yourself from all manner of social obligations by using the fear as your reason. Back then when our nights out might spiral into two-day sessions where friends' groups swapped in and out like tag-team wrestlers and involved traversing the whole city while having the same conversation with a revolving cast of strangers and pals, it was normal that someone might disappear into their own personal quarantine between Monday and Friday. We let that sleeping dog lie.

We fell into dark psychological holes and sustained ourselves on chipper chips, cans of Coke and Lion bars, avoiding housemates like drunk drivers avoid checkpoints. It was even normal to get an SOS from the depths. This was strange, because as a bunch we were all tough when it came to our feelings. We only shared emotionally when

we were high or drunk; the rest of the time our friend-
ship was a lot like policing. We monitored each other's
behaviour and made our judgement known when we
didn't approve. 'The state of you'; 'Stop shiteing on';
'Go on out of that,' etc., etc.

So whenever we got a message from someone who was
going through the fear, we recognised that it was really bad.
And we responded seriously: 'It's the fear. Don't worry. It's
all in your head.'

The fear *is* all in your head.

For a bunch of underfed party kids who were so desen-
sitised to ourselves and our inner worlds that we could fall
asleep to music played at 160 bpm, this was a valuable and
unexpected piece of wisdom.

Many of us come to meditation thinking that it'll
bring an end to the personal hell that our life's become, but
here's a thing: the fastest way out of hell is through misery.
Meditation is often not the end of the fear, it's actually just
the beginning. We can spend an entire life shirking away
from fears, but when we understand that fear is something we're carrying in our head, the only solution is to
accept it and explore it and ask it to show itself, over and
over again. This is the work of meditation. It's the art of
throwing away all your mental crutches, all your comforts

and all your distractions and facing the great waves of fear that inevitably arrive when we examine our lives. It takes phenomenal courage. Even reading this book does. This book contains many inconvenient truths. Meditation is not some sweet, blissed-out ride on a cushion, it's a cold shower on the most Monday of Monday mornings.

I used to drink every day. I used to take great pride in how much and how fast I could drink, but I hardly drink anything these days. When I do, you can bet someone's just got married or someone's been buried, or I've landed a book deal. Outside those times, it's rare to find me really drinking. But I used to drink a lot. I loved it. I woke up on mornings when I knew I would be sinking pints that evening with a beatific smile on my face. One of the first great fears I encountered when I began to meditate was the fear that it would make me quit alcohol. I knew that my spiritual life could not also contain my spirits life. I'm not saying there's anything wrong with alcohol, but if there are situations in your life when you can't be without it, you're missing out on an opportunity for growth.

A voice in the stillness of my meditation would tell me that my relationship with booze wasn't serving me any more. It didn't fit with the newfound joy I was cultivating. And a louder voice, a voice that sounded like deep laughter, would reply, 'But where will you find friends? What will you do in the evenings? How will you handle dinner parties, events, the sesh, Christmas without a drink in your hand?' In the end it just disappeared without me trying. My love for heavy drinking went out with a whimper. There wasn't even a cinematic downing of all the booze in the house. It was still there. I just didn't want it any more.

As you set out along this path, parts of you fade away. In a sense, you lose a little bit of yourself. Your habits. Your patterns. Some friends are hard to be around. You begin to question if they're actually good for you. You begin to question a lot, actually. I remember coming back from one of my first retreats and not listening to music for what seemed like a whole month. There was no music that could improve the silence, so I didn't play it.

This is scary. The things that were central to your identity might move into the background. It feels a little like the earth beneath you has slipped or that you're you, but not really you. Your way of talking might change and you'll experience fear. The only way to handle this fear is to embrace it wholeheartedly. You can't put the peel back on an orange, right?

Once you've woken up just a little, it's almost impossible to put yourself back to sleep again. And this brings with it even more fear, because you know that there's still so much more to come. More change, more confronting yourself, more shedding of skin.

But as we begin to explore the fears we carry around in our own heads, a realisation dawns: we are all experiencing more or less the same life. None of us knows what direction to go in. We really do know nothing. Even the wise ones, the ones who sit in silence in their caves, have moments of brainless confusion. Monks have nervous breakdowns too. Life is a kind of constant insecurity. The fear you experience after a night out, when you're raw, sensitive, exposed and depleted of minerals and hydration, is just an amplification of the fear that surrounds us at all times.

There's an old folk story about a young girl. She's training to be a warrior in some ancient fantasy warrior school, and today is her final test. For this test she has to fight the one thing in the world she's most afraid of, and for her this is fear itself. So she goes into the battle ring and there's fear, and as expected he's big and ugly and oh so scary. The young warrior walks right up to him and very politely asks, 'Do you mind if I fight you?'

Fear's a little taken aback. Folks don't normally talk to him, let alone talk to him politely.

'Little girl,' he says, 'of course you can fight me. And because you've been so nice, you can ask me anything you like.'

The little girl is brave, but she's also smart. 'Okay,' she says, 'how do I defeat you?'

'It's easy,' fear says. 'I don't actually have any power. All I do is get up in your face and confuse you, and when you're confused you do what I say. If you can remain calm then I'm powerless.'

This is just a folk story, but that doesn't make the following less true: if you can remain calm, then fear is powerless.

Exercise: Fear

Think of all the moments in life when you grew the most. The experiences when you really overcame something. Quite often those moments involved lots of fear, yet you survived. Look at you, here now, reading a book, and that time is now in your past.

Fear is very natural. It's the door we have to go through to allow ourselves to change. The more comfortable you can become with fear, and more specifically facing it, the more you can invite change into your life.

What are the things you are afraid of doing now?

Write them down. Even in the margin of this book. I don't mind, it's paid for now.

How different would your life be if you had the courage to confront these fears, to grasp life despite being scared?

So What?

Nothing happens. Nobody comes, nobody goes. It's awful.

— SAMUEL BECKETT

To really do nothing, with perfection, is as difficult as doing everything.

— ALAN WATTS

Meditation is heavily reliant on sky and water imagery. Big waves disturb our balance and dark clouds obscure our minds. Rain storms gather and then they pass, and then they gather again. Look at any meditation book. They're all following the same design brief. Christ, look at this book even, I just signed away all rights, so for all I know the cover might be a blue sky, over a blue lake, surrounded by blue heather.

When you do buy books on meditation there's a strong chance the cover is blue like the sky. Meditation teachers would be left scratching their heads if we didn't have blue skies and weather fronts. Maybe we'd have to use the analogy of spam. Your mind is a cleanly cached website and thoughts are the advertising pop-ups and the spam. Or your mind is like a YouTube algorithm, throwing suggestions your way that vaguely relate to your tastes but are definitely not something you want to watch.

So weather imagery is useful for the meditation teacher and the student because before you can actually see the benefits of meditation you need to believe in them, if only just a little bit, and everyone believes in bad weather.

It's so much easier with psychedelics. With psychedelics, there are lights and sounds, and occasionally your whole body dissolves. There are bad memories too. Darkness, trauma, things you'd rather not see. Music sounds better, your body feels like it has extra limbs. It really is quite the show. I witnessed my own rebirth on the floor of a small hut in South Africa once, but that's a tale for another book if they'll let me. All these wild things can happen with meditation too, but a lot of the time – actually most of the time – nothing at all is happening. Psychedelics do all the work for you; with meditation you're doing all the work on your own. And sometimes you wonder what you're doing the work for.

This is why belief is so important. I'm not talking about gullibly following each and every instruction, but if you approach meditation with a closed and cynical mind, it might not do anything for you. You run the risk of opening your eyes after five minutes, and saying 'So what?' I've had that on a few occasions with people, and the only piece of advice I can give is this: nobody can walk the path for you. The 'so what' stage can last an entire lifetime. I hope in your case that it won't.

Meditation doesn't always land. You might be one of these 'so what' people yourself. Before I finally bit the bullet and started doing this every day, I was that guy. I'd tried a few guided meditations but, to be honest, I thought they all just sounded creepy. Speak up, get to the point, not another west coast American. I was one of those people who said things like 'Jogging is my meditation' or 'Tidying the house is my meditation.' I have always been slightly OCD. I make Marie Kondo look like a slob. If tidying the house was my meditation, I've have levitated off this planet a long time ago. But it's not. Meditation is meditation. And to do that you need a little belief and a lot of patience.

We don't enjoy being patient. It feels patronising to even write the word. The problem with so much meditation guidance is that it sounds like the things your parents might have said to you when you were in the car going on holiday, and couldn't deal with the suspense any more. My parents liked to play with us. They didn't tell us we were going on holiday until we were in the car and a good distance along the road. That was great. My god, did we shriek with delight. But sometimes, my dad would do it the other way round and say we're going on holiday, when actually we weren't, and that was horrible. Every time we got in the car as a family I didn't know if we were going to west Cork or to get the ear wax washed out at the doctor's. To this day, no matter who's driving, I'm a nervous passenger.

I hope this doesn't come across like I don't like my parents. They made me who I am and for that I love them dearly, but as you begin to explore the decisions you've made, the habits you've adopted, the triggers that set you off and so on, the trail will inevitably lead back to them. The same thing happens when you go to therapy. You begin to hate your father, then you begin to hate your mother, then slowly you begin to understand them both, and along the way understand yourself too. If the therapist is good, and you're prepared to let go of a lot of anger, you might even end up loving your parents like you did when you were a tiny child again. It's possible. I do.

Meditation is the art of doing nothing, and that's a tough sell. We're doers by nature, but meditation is an invitation to just be and wait. It's like watching paint dry, or grass grow. Very little happens for a very long time.

And this requires patience. Oodles and oodles of patience. We are not a patient people. Humans, in general, are not comfortable with patience. This is another thing we can blame on whoever came up with the design for our brains. Those devices are built to respond to the environment around us, and the environment around us these days is late-stage capitalism, where everything's been monetised to death and the things we used to enjoy for free are sold back to us as services, and most of us, nearly all of us, are somewhat miserable. It's hard to be patient in this environment when all the prompts we're receiving are build, grow, expand, rebrand, more, more, more.

There are many occasions in life when the need to be patient is thrown at us. Getting sick is the most obvious one. When things fall apart is another. When we're falling in love but they're not replying within a minute of you receiving their 'read' receipt. When we're caught in a pandemic.

I became very busy during the first weeks of Covid-19. It was good for business. Folks who ordinarily would never have meditated were contacting me asking for help. We'd meditate and then talk and all of them were experiencing this bizarre external pressure to use the pandemic as an opportunity to reinvent themselves, rebrand a business, learn a new language, upskill and so on.

'It might be more useful to learn to like yourself,' I'd say.

In every situation when we're forced to practise patience, we're asked to examine our relationship with this present moment, and if we're honest, we'll say it's like sitting on a hot stove. Albert Einstein said that: 'When you sit with a nice girl for two hours you think it's only a minute, but when you sit on a hot stove for a minute you think it's two hours. That's relativity.'

It's very hard to convince someone to sit still, and do more or less nothing for ten minutes. People want to sweat, they want to feel gains, they want to scale up. Meditation is an objectless pursuit. It's the art of being okay with nothing. But being okay with nothing doesn't sound very appealing to our goal-driven brains. It sounds a lot like the prize every kid gets just because they took part, even the one who forgot their sports gear and had to watch from the side. Our brains were designed to keep us busy. A busy little *Homo sapiens* gathered enough nuts, caught enough fish and generally remembered everybody's names at caveman quiz night, and this kept her alive. This busyness has been useful for us, but it's not made us happy.

If you want to be happy you have to be patient. If you want to meditate you have to be patient. Patience is the art of not getting anywhere, and our patience is tested in the very first minute of every meditation. You sit down, and the first instruction is to wait for the breath, and depending upon how agitated your mind is or the environment around you, it can seem like the breath never comes. Or if it does come, it can seem so inconsequential and so boring and so what. Without patience our tendency is to remember something that we should be doing that's more important than meditation. We'll remember an email that we haven't replied to. Or perhaps we'll remember an argument we had last week and think now is the time to replay it, now is the time to come up with a better reply. It's all staircase wit in the meditation world. Patience is the difference between you finding your feet in meditation or falling at the first hurdle.

The problem with patience is that it seems like it's the second word out of every adult's mouth when we're growing up. Being a child is basically the art of learning that you can't have what you want right now. For us it was the patience to wait until the news was over so we could watch *The Simpsons*. Or the patience to make it through a plate of mushy peas so we could eat the Viennetta. And, as we got older, the patience to wait until the slow set at the GAA disco so you could get to dance with a girl.

As boys we sometimes used to talk about how our lives would be when we left school. We'd drive Porsche 911s and have beautiful wives and own our own companies. I don't know where these ideas came from. We grew up on roads where Porsche 911s couldn't go or they'd be hopped off by a pothole into the ditch. I don't know where the beautiful wives were coming from either, considering none of us had even had a girlfriend yet.

None of us really enjoyed school. I belonged to a small gang of puny guys who didn't play GAA. The boys who did were the gods of the school. They were allowed to skip classes. The teachers called them by their first names, while the rest of us were addressed by our surnames. For no reason other than they were somewhat skilled at repeating one skill over and over again for 70 minutes, these boys were elevated to another level.

And so we learned from that young age to be patient. Life, which wasn't fair when we were children, and was again proving to be a bit of a clunker during school, was bound to be better once we got out of this kip. But then we did, and it wasn't.

You can't force patience, just as you can't tell someone to relax and expect them to do it. But by dropping deep into the feeling of being impatient we can pick apart why it's so uncomfortable for us. When we're impatient we're not happy with reality as it is. We're like the child crying because it's raining outside, but we're all meant to be grown up now, aren't we?

As we begin to dissect impatience we get to see that its heart is anger, and the heart of anger is pain. The pain is our disconnect from the present. It's a kind of heartbreak, really. We spend our lives so focused on the future and the past that the present moment, this forced present moment when we're standing in a long queue, or stuck in traffic, or being told that 'Your call is important to us, so please stay on the line' can be painful. The present is reality and when we recognise how uncomfortable we are with reality, we can begin to understand why our lives are so unsatisfactory.

We used to holiday in caravans and tents all around the southwest of Ireland. On some days it was grim. Rainwater crept inside the canvas. There were endless afternoons of sitting around plastic tables, playing Jack Change It, Pick Up, poker with matchsticks, where my dad came away with all the matches, all the time. So many of these summers felt like accelerated training courses in advanced patience.

Impatience is a wonderful teacher, and patience is the sign that you're learning. Being okay with the present is the secret to surviving Earth. Saying 'So what?' every time you're presented with something new, or a different approach, or a challenge to your beliefs is just our way of putting this important work on the long finger. Eventually you'll have to reconcile with the present. Meditation is all about being okay with reality as it is rather than how you want it to be. It's about being patient to the point where the waiting is no longer painful, where every moment is an opportunity for exploration and growth.

Most people only get to do this when they become terminally ill. For many people this pandemic has been a great simulator of what it's like to be terminally ill – no travel, no movement, no plans. A radical intervention that's made us all very aware of the present. A unique opportunity to explore what lies beyond boredom and encourage the empowering insight that only appears when we stop saying 'So what?' and just sit there.

Exercise: Patience

Our intolerance for the present moment comes to a head whenever we're forced to be patient. Waiting is basically a type of uneasy relationship with now. It creeps up on us all the time, but perhaps the way to beat impatience at its own game is to factor it in. Explore it.

When clients come to me for one-on-one sessions, quite often we'll discover that they never let themselves rest. From morning to night, they keep going, working on to-dos, putting out fires, solving problems. If we talk further, we'll realise that the problems never really end. You solve one, and another emerges. The problems are a matter of perspective.

To confront this, I set them a task. Schedule half an hour every day or every other day, or if this seems incredibly daunting every three days. In this half an hour, don't plan anything, don't tidy the house, don't be near your devices, don't talk to a friend. This half an hour is just a test to see how comfortable or uncomfortable you can be in your own skin, waiting patiently for half an hour.

What happens when you schedule time for nothing, I mean when you schedule time to just practise patience, is that creativity emerges. Creativity is linked to our intuition and intuition is accessed through patience.

Change and the Irish Summer

Those who cannot change their minds cannot change anything.

> — GEORGE BERNARD SHAW

Do you want to be right? It's not difficult to be right, but you will be right and alone.

> — ESTHER PEREL

If you haven't already noticed, and if you haven't I'd beg you now to try, everything around you – your friends, your family, your home, the plants outside, the trees, even your body and its thoughts and feelings – are all subject to change. Every single thing on this planet is changing, and changing constantly.

In Buddhism this is called *anicca*. It means that nothing lasts and nothing stays the same, and it's probably the most important takeaway from this entire book. If you can get that, if you can fully understand it and then remember it as you venture through this great simulator called life, you're sorted. It means you're no longer clinging and grasping at things, you're flowing. To be human is to be like flowing water. Or, in our case, falling rain.

If you're meditating, you're seeing the world as it really is. It's a dose of reality. It's not a magic trick. It's just bringing your attention to your breath, sitting back and enjoying the show, without taking part in the whole drama of judging it.

A show?

You know when you go to a film and there are moments when you forget you're actually watching a film? You feel like you're really in the film. Then someone beside you gets a message on their phone, or the guy behind you kicks your seat, and you're pulled out of the movie for a second and reminded that you're just a spectator. Okay, wait for it. Your thoughts are just like watching a movie, while believing you are the movie. Meditation is the gentle kick in the back reminding you that you're not. Everything is constantly changing and if you're not constantly aware of this, you will invite constant suffering into your life.

This too will pass.

I've met about half a dozen people who have this tattooed on their arms. And it's so true. Except for tattoos, though – get a bad one of those and it never passes.

Meditation is not about sucking the joy out of things, but it's definitely about understanding the reality of pleasure and the reality of pain. Both will pass, both change. Death is the only certainty, and depending on how far you go down this rabbit hole that is the spiritual life, you might even begin to think of death as something you've been through many times before. Just another sunset, in many lifetimes of many sunsets.

A warning. You might come to meditation hoping to sleep better at night, but you could leave telling people at the office Christmas party about your theory on past lives and rebirths, and all kinds of mad out-there shit. Don't fret, they will almost certainly be drunk and won't remember.

But think about sunset. We accept that the sun sets. You'd be considered pretty hysterical if you started wailing every time the sun started going down. Most of us have let go of clinging to daylight. If we didn't, each day would be a terrible tragedy. After seven o'clock, or eight, or even nine, depending on where you are in the world, and what time of year it is, you'd begin to hear the wailing, and know, ah, the sun must be setting again, the very sensitive folks are crying.

This is a funny example. Nobody's actually crying every day the sun sets, but we do cry all the time when things, that we know will end, end. Something to think about, right? When we forget this, we suffer. Take love, for example. Love can be a real kick in the nuts if you don't fully appreciate and brace for change. If you don't believe me, just examine some Boyzone song titles:

'Will I Ever See You Again?'

'Can't Stop Thinking About You'

'Nothing Without You'

'When Will You Understand'

'Just Can't Say Goodbye'.

We are kinda ridiculous the way we approach romance. This is the beautiful naivety of us humans. Our frail core, always looking for something permanent, something solid, when we live in a world made up of micro-vibrations and inaccurate perceptions.

Change is the water we swim in every day, yet we feel affronted whenever it happens to us.

'I broke up with Mary.'

'No way, why?'

'I dunno, she just changed.'

If your partner doesn't change within the span of your relationship, do check beneath their scalp while they're sleeping – they might be an AI.

Or worse, what about the times when we promise each other that we won't change? And sure maybe we mean it, but we're deluded nonetheless. You've lost that loving feeling? Well of course you have, it would be contrary to all natural laws if you hadn't.

It's a feeling, right? Like thoughts, they come and go, and come and go. This is not to say you should delete all your apps or break up with your partner, but just consider the demands you're putting on your romantic relationships. *Anicca* means nothing lasts for ever, nothing stays the same. This doesn't mean that love dies, but it certainly doesn't stay the exact same, and the way to keep it going is to recognise that and put your energy into reinventing and adapting to the change. Fall in love with the same person again and again and again, if you can.

In school, we used to say, 'The loose nail gets hammered.' It was meant as a threat. Don't step out of line. Don't change. In truth, if we humans really were nails, we'd all be loose. Being loose is really the only way to get through life.

Resistance to change is the number one cause of sadness among humans. I'm at that age now where the men around me are turning grey. I'm turning grey too. Each haircut throws a few new ones up, but at least I'm not losing my hair yet. I know a lot of men who are. They hide their shortage under hats. Woollen beanies that generate heat like a combustion engine. You see them in the summer, out by the canal, in the park, at a festival, their brains slowly cooking inside tea cosy hats. I don't blame them. We have created a society that doesn't value ageing, a society that would prefer to ignore change and hide it under a tea cosy. But imagine if we did. Imagine if we could look on grey hairs as signs of experience; baldness and plumpness as symbols of wisdom, years under the belt; crow's feet as military stripes.

Or if we could see plans for what they are: nothing more than just hopes that we're casting into the wind. Buddhists hate hope. Hope is a desire that the future will be different; again, it's a kind of uneasiness with the present. The way to be at ease with the present is to be adaptive. We can plan all we like, but in the end all we can really do is adapt. This is how water flows, and how we can too.

Ajahn Chah was a Thai meditation teacher. He had a monastery deep in the woods where he and his fellow monks lived a pretty simple life. They ate just once a day. They begged for alms. For kicks they'd do these all-night vigils where they'd just sit in the meditation hall until seven the next morning, following their breath. They were, in the language of my youth, hardcore. Hardcore people know things. Ajahn Chah was an expert on change. He used to tell a story about an ornate cup that he had. Having an ornate drinking vessel and being a monk is a big deal. Monks have pretty much nothing. That's the deal. So to him a decorative cup was like a Lear jet to you and me. Chah used to say that while he admired the cup, and enjoyed the cup, and liked drinking from it when he did, for him the cup was already broken. If he were to turn suddenly one day and knock it onto the ground, so that it smashed into a million tiny pieces, he wouldn't go, 'Oh shit'; instead he'd go, 'Well of course, this already happened a long long time ago.'

This is the lesson of change. We can see it in ourselves every day. We can watch it from the dry side of the window during a typical Irish summer. Summers that are sometimes great for us, but are mostly great for ducks. Change is the water ducks and humans swim in.

I feel proud that in my lifetime I got to take part in two incredible changes in Irish law. In one we got to overturn an injustice that prevented gay couples from enjoying the freedoms that straight couples had. And in another, we cancelled the law that forbade women choosing what to do with their own bodies. When I think of it now I'm shocked. Change happened at an unprecedented level. And when it did it reached places we'd never have imagined. My mother supported marriage equality. She's a Christian. When I was growing up, she threw a copy of the

Red Hot Chili Peppers' *Blood Sugar Sex Magik* on the fire, saying that the lyrics were satanic. Satan, yes, but Anthony Kiedis too, Mum.

We all have personal stories of people changing. You can never imagine who might become an ally. Change is a gift. Nothing is set in stone, least of all you.

Right now I'm working on this chapter while at the same time jumping to my Twitter feed where human rights protests are kicking off in America, Hong Kong and Belarus. The protests are an example of what happens when inevitable change meets resistance. Protests are what happens when societies don't take care of their problems, when we try to preserve old, unfair modes of doing. They are symbolic of the conflict we experience at a personal level, in our heads, every single day when we don't accept the natural law of change.

The one thing that stands in the way of our personal change and our societal change is ignorance. In Buddhism the term for ignorance is *moha*. It's considered a poison. Ignorance is when we believe that things won't change and when we fight to prevent that change, and bring misery into our own lives and the lives of the people around us. We are meditating to come out of our ignorance, to cast a bright light on the shadows that prevent us from growing up and to bring peace into our lives and the lives of the people around us.

I'll let James Baldwin, the African-American author, play this chapter out:

'It is certain, in any case, that ignorance, allied with power, is the most ferocious enemy justice can have.'

Exercise: Understanding your own ignorance

It can be useful to doubt everything you believe and think. If our thoughts and feelings are not to be trusted, why do we place so much trust in the things we believe? Why do we get into arguments and then defend our position so fiercely that we act out and scream at people who we actually love and care about? People we would defend immediately if someone else was screaming at them.

A good way to observe your own ignorance is to try and put yourself in the other person's shoes as often as possible, and especially in an argument.

This is extremely difficult to do, especially when you're being triggered, but if you can maintain some of your focus on your breath while you're arguing, if you can recognise the triggers and protect yourself, you can stay calm.

Ignorance makes us believe that there's only one right way. Life is much more nuanced than that. Life is much more watery, much murkier. The more we can interpret things from other perspectives, the more we can challenge our ignorance.

Challenging your ignorance, like all things to do with your personality, is not a one-treatment fix. You have to be constantly vigilant, constantly aware and constantly tending to what is coming up in you. This is how we bring harmony into our lives.

Notions and the Self

Despite appearances, I am just as ordinary, just as unremarkable and just as human as you are.

— PANTI BLISS

And the truth is, we are all basically the universe – pretending to be humans for a brief moment of time.

— RUPAUL

When you commit to meditation, you're committing to a process of self-annihilation that doesn't stop until you finally find the part of you that can't be destroyed. It might surprise you to know that the part of you that can't be destroyed is not the ego, it's actually a thing called awareness. Awareness is not exclusive to meditation. We drop into it on many different occasions in our life. It happens in nature, when we're looking out across the sea, or when we make our way to a mountain top and look down, and maybe the gods are on your side and, this once, the view's not blocked by mist, clouds and a coming downpour. Awareness is something we're very familiar with. When we discover it in meditation, it's often like revisiting a memory, or déjà vu. We round a corner and think, hold on, I know this place, I know it really well. This place is called no-self, which doesn't mean that you don't exist but that your small, limited concept of existence is not real.

You know the word *namaste*? They say it at the end of yoga classes. It's sometimes written on the bottom of the menu in Indian restaurants. Sometimes it's even the name of the place. It means 'the divine in me bows down to the divine in you'. It's basically saying that there's a spark of something special in you that's also in me. How cool. Nice to meet you.

This spark is also just awareness. It's the place we come to when we pull back from thinking our thoughts and begin observing them instead. Awareness is not neutral. The reason it feels so familiar to us is because when we find ourselves in a state of awareness, it opens our hearts, so we also find ourselves in a state of love. The two go together. To be completely aware is to feel love, Donna Summer style.

When you sit with yourself, and that means when you stop distracting yourself for long enough to actually see what's going on, you begin to unpeel like an onion. The first layer to go is the sense that you know anything. The longer you sit in silence the more often you'll be hit over the head by your own ignorance. Confronting your bias is the psychological experiment equivalent of the TV show *This Is Your Life*. Except you're not happy to see any of the guests who come out on stage. Many of them, in fact, are super embarrassing. I'm the bully? I'm the bad friend? I was the one who didn't listen in the relationship? Some people don't enjoy meditating or any inquiry work for this exact reason. It's challenging as all hell.

The second layer to go is all the strata of negativity that you've gathered over the years. The limiting beliefs, the neuroses, the depression. This is a deep excavation. We carry much of this negativity from birth, and we carry it so long we forget that we can put it back down again. Your dad called you dumb when you were growing up and thirty years later you're still calling yourself dumb – that kind of thing.

The third layer is your notions of self. These are our carefully constructed stories: 'I am Conor, I like this and that, I am good at tidying a house but terrible at cooking, I am not very confident and I hate speaking in public, I don't dance.' If you sit long enough you might discover that the sense that we are in some way a passenger behind an imaginary wheel inside our heads is a total illusion. Everything that happens, every thought, every action, is part of a process involving multiple neurons; there is no single self that is carried on from one moment to the next, although it feels like there is.

Have you ever taken psychedelics? There are moments in the middle of the psychedelic experience where this veil of self collapses and we realise that we're nothing more than the experience around us. In some religions they call this moment transcendence. In Buddhism it's the concept of no-self. It's not something you need to concern yourself with every day. After all, the conventional self has a use. I'm writing this book; I'm sending the manuscript to the editor; I'm trying hard to avoid checking the Instagram post I made fifteen minutes ago.

As you dive deeper into the process, be prepared for this development. Be prepared to lose this sense of self a little. This is what happens when the sense of self loosens its grip:

Someone will talk shit about you, and it won't cause you any offence.

You'll start listening more than talking.

People will leave your life and instead of thinking 'How could they?', you'll think 'So be it.'

A driver will cut you off and you'll feel no need for revenge.

You'll care less how you appear.

You'll go out in public and not think that all eyes are on you.

You'll post on social media and not delete the post five minutes later in a fit of heightened self-awareness.

You'll forgive.

You'll laugh at yourself.

You'll no longer look for internal stability outside yourself.

You'll change profoundly and regularly.

You'll stop taking yourself so seriously.

You'll speak your mind.

You'll drop your notions.

Personal development is a lot like gardening. You uproot weeds and sometimes they grow back again. And sometimes they're gone for good. There's no real way to be sure, so instead we have to be vigilant. We approach the layers of our own particular onion with the idea that our work will never end. And as we're vigilant we'll occasionally notice the layers slipping and realise that all we are is awareness, and all that awareness is, is love.

If you're noticing resistance in yourself right now, a resistance to the word 'love', a resistance to the vague concept of awareness, a resistance to something new, then that's just proof that the ego is in fine working order. The ego is there to maintain the status quo. Good job. Come back in another 10,000 kilometres.

You don't have to destroy your ego in order to make progress in meditation, but you do have to learn some workarounds.

We work around the ego by healing ourselves. People who are completely healed have barely a trace of ego. I've not met many people like that, but we all have the ability. There was a woman where I grew up who fed the poor kids in my school. She'd invite them in for a bowl of soup or a boiled potato or something. Her smile was the same whoever she met. She glowed like a light bulb. At the time of writing we don't have devices that can measure the level of ego in a person. But if we did, if smart folks in white lab coats had engineered some technology that could look beneath the cranium and detect levels of ego, I'll bet it would find that she had less than a trace. There was something exceptional about that woman. She had truly embraced her best side. She had found that spark that unites us all and fed it diligently. All the best and worst qualities you can imagine are in us. Some are vibrant and some are dormant. Who you become depends very simply on what you feed.

There's an old Native American story about a grand-mother talking to her grandchild. She tells the child, 'There are two wolves doing battle in my heart right now. One is a wolf of anger and bitterness and jealousy, and the other is a wolf of love and forgiveness and empathy.' The kid asks, 'Granny, which one is going to win?' The grandmother replies, 'Whichever one I feed.'

We get the same option every time an emotion, a thought or a feeling arises. Do I identify with it, or can I just let it go? And the more we let it go, the more this sense of ego, this sense of self, loses its grip upon us. Thoughts are just passing by, after all. It's your decision to stop them in their tracks and not let them go.

In Buddhism, attachment to the self is an affliction. Thinking from an 'I' or 'me' perspective is a recipe for illness. Understanding that there is no independent self, and that we're all interconnected, might just be the one thing that saves our species.

The ego was originally supposed to be the part of us that combined our nature and nurture, and made deci-sions based upon reasoning. The suffering arises when we become ego-focused, and instead of expanding and blossoming, our awareness shrinks and we become selfish. The more 'I' am the most important thing in the world, and the more focus put upon 'me', the more pressure 'I' feel, because it seems as though the whole world revolves around 'me'. Any disruption or upset that occurs is felt to be much bigger than it really is, because an ego-focused person's world is far smaller than a less ego-focused person's world. People with smaller egos feel more connected to the outside world because they're less focused on themselves.

The most consistent job I've had in my life has been as a bartender. I must have worked in about twenty different places all over the world. Bartenders are the great listeners of the world, but we're also great enablers. We sell alcohol to people who clearly have addiction problems with it. I spent so many nights counselling barflies, while trying to get them to leave, because it was after midnight and I wanted to get home. So many nights, until I realised that I was part of the problem and retrained as a barista, which felt more wholesome but to be honest was zero craic.

The thing you notice, over and over again, from talking to the last person to leave any bar is this: we all have sad stories to tell. We're all fighting personal battles every day. This constructed idea of self we have feels so solid, so unmoveable, and so inescapable that it's no wonder people would beg me for one more drink rather than go home and be with themselves.

No-self is one of the most hopeful of all the Buddhist teachings. It means that everything associated with the self is an illusion. There is no fixed you, so there's no reason for self-criticism, self-recrimination or self-centredness.

No-self means, very simply, that we can go home at night and sleep easy in the knowledge that we are constantly remaking ourselves, constantly starting over, and that my pain, my objects, my pride and my reputation are just mental constructions that grow from my thoughts. And at this stage in the book, you don't need reminding to not believe your thoughts.

Exercise: Discovering no-self

At this stage you've probably gathered that every instruction in this book begins with 'Sit down on your own somewhere quiet.' I could probably have just called the book that. I could have written an entire book with that line repeated on every page.

Trying to locate your 'self' – the driver behind the wheel in your body, so to speak – is a very interesting exercise. You can do it by setting a timer for five minutes with a repeating sound every 30 or 60 seconds. Each time the sound rings, try to locate the part of you that is receiving that sound. Not your ears, just the part of you, the self, that is experiencing the sound.

It doesn't matter if you do or don't get this the first time. Like everything else in this book, it's all experimental, and we all come at this from different places, different starting points.

This exercise is just a suggestion. Can you find the real centre of attention in yourself, and if you can't – that is, if you can't find the self; if, as many experienced meditators and a good number of scientists say, it doesn't exist – then why are we all so self-conscious?

Are You Satisfied with Yourself Now?

You're on Earth. There's no cure for that.

— SAMUEL BECKETT

The true value of a human being is determined primarily by the measure and sense in which he has attained liberation from the self.

— ALBERT EINSTEIN

A problem with teaching spirituality is that it can sound like a lot of smartarsery. It's obscure, it's intangible, there's some person telling a story about a wild ox; no, a monkey; no, wait, now she's trying to ask me to imagine the sound of one hand clapping. The stories don't always land because life and its lessons are experiential. Awakening is a skill that you don't learn in a book, you really learn it on the job. The deep learning comes as you observe your own experiences. All this is mere foreshadowing. But seeing as we find ourselves in a book, here's a story anyway.

It's an old Indian one about three blind men who encounter an elephant for the first time. Each of them approaches the elephant, who you can only imagine was a very chill animal, or just chained to something solid, and they begin to touch it in order to work out what it might be. One blind man grabs it by the tusk. 'Okay,' he said, 'an elephant is like a snake, only harder.' The second blind man grabs it by the tail – this animal might have been sedated – 'Aha! An elephant is like a rope.' The third man grabs the elephant by the ear and exclaims, 'No, you're both wrong. I know it, an elephant is like a fan.'

This story isn't a joke about people fumbling round a huge animal; it's a parable, a way to see into ourselves. The parable is about truth, and how relative it is. The bigger picture is never revealed to us completely, and the minute you think you've really got it is the minute before you realise you haven't got it at all. What you believe today will be challenged tomorrow and possibly broken next week. This is also *anicca*. You change, I change, even the picture changes.

This is why monks are silent. At one level it's because they like it, at another because they don't get out much so they don't have movies or parties to chat about, but at another they know that if they open their mouth it just increases the chances of them getting it all wrong.

When Buddha taught, he said very little too. The guy was concise. He didn't want to leave room for misinterpretation and, I feel, he didn't want a religion and a cult of personality to develop after his death, but there's very little you can do to protect your own reputation after you're gone. Just ask what Samuel Beckett thinks about all the gyms around the world with the banner 'Fail Better', coated in a thick film of hard-earned sweat, pinned in front of the treadmills.

Buddha's signature teaching was this: Life on the whole is unsatisfactory. The root cause of all our problems is wanting life to be satisfying all the time. Understanding that it's not is the way to be okay. This is called *dukkha*, and in fairness it's a bit of a buzzkill to begin with.

Dukkha means that life is unsatisfactory and it's the foundation on which all Buddhist teachings are based. If you feel that life is 100% satisfactory, you would never have picked up this book. You probably wouldn't be reading at all. You'd just be sitting there, transfixed, staring into space with a big grin on your face while crowds of country folk, up for the day, gathered round and took selfies with you.

The problem with Buddha's truth is that it runs contrary to what society teaches us. As we race along, through childhood and into adulthood, and on into our dotage, we can find, if we look hard enough, that we're never really here – we're time-travelling. We're living for the weekend, we're remembering better times, we're waiting for our prince to come, we're counting down the days to our next holiday. All we are experiencing is the present, but our thoughts dwell in the future or the past.

I spent the first few decades of my life time-travelling. When I was growing up in Kildare I wanted to be in Dublin. When I got to Dublin, I wanted to be in California, and the last time I was in California I felt so homesick for Kildare that there were times when I'd look at the burritos and horchata in front of me and wish I was sipping milky tea and eating white bread sandwiches in my grandmother's back garden in Clane.

We're all time-travellers until something nails us to the present. We get nailed to the present when we get a phone call from the hospital with the results of our biopsy, or when our partner of many years unexpectedly announces that they're leaving, or when we pass a building in flames. I remember walking past the Shelbourne Hotel one evening when it was being evacuated for a fire. I had just finished a bar shift and I was tired. I was walking home with a chicken tikka baguette and a strawberry Yop. There were about a dozen fire engines outside, and confused people in robes gathered round the front of the building. On the other side of the street, in front of the green, were about a hundred people all nailed to the spot. We looked at each other in amazement. A complete stranger offered me a Silk Cut. Someone joked, 'Good luck to them evacuating the bar.' Our time-travelling devices were temporarily grounded.

The reason we are so rarely in the present is because we spend our entire lives running away from the present. The present is tricky. Being in the present is painful. The present is where we confront the demons. And it's only when we are fully in the present that we fully capture the inherent unsatisfactoriness of life. This is the *dukkha* that Buddha talked about.

Before I ever meditated I had many misconceptions about meditation. I thought that it was, for the most part, a bunch of gentle yet annoying people sitting in circles thinking positive thoughts. They'd opted out of life. They'd opted out of the dissatisfaction that I was experiencing all the time. They were escaping from the misery. Back then I was doing a pretty good job at producing misery. I was a troubled little man. I'd love to bring him back some time. I'd love to load him up in the same way you might play your wedding video from ten years ago. Just to watch and remember.

One time, my anxiety got so out of hand that it manifested in an eating disorder. I was living in the south of Italy, working a teaching job at a university when all of a sudden every time I ate in public, the food would get stuck in my throat, and I'd get the sudden urge to vomit. Sfogliatella, linguine alle vongole, pizza margherita, caffè alla nocciola, it was all the same. If someone was in eyeshot, I couldn't swallow. If I could sense eyes anywhere, I couldn't swallow. Madonna santa! My solution was to not eat in public any more. I refused all dinner invites, all lunch offers, all food festivals, saints' days, street parties and street vendors. I became a secret eater. Months later I took a summer job in London, and whatever I'd been experiencing passed. It just disappeared. A change of perspective killed it off.

I once knew an alcoholic chef from New Orleans who had to leave the city when he quit alcohol because, he said, there was simply nothing to do if you weren't out getting wasted. In Italy, denied the opportunity to join others at the table, there was also simply nothing to do. But I sometimes try to bring that version of me back. I try to recreate the feeling of utter dread whenever a colleague invited me to a birthday, and know that even though I was saying yes in the moment, I'd eventually be making up an excuse and flaking on the night.

Back then I would have loved to opt out of life's dissatisfaction, only I didn't know how, and whenever I encountered signs and teachers, I was never ready. You can grow comfortable in your dissatisfaction. It's easy to get used to feeling bad and then become attached to that. To a hammer, all things are nails. To victims, every gesture can seem like an attack. Pain, like every other strong distracting sensation, can be addictive.

But when I began my own journey I realised that meditation involved just as much pain as non-meditation, but less of the illusion. Pain occurs whenever the illusion that life is comfortable and controllable breaks. Pain occurs when things don't go to plan. It doesn't have to be an eating disorder. Dissatisfaction is everywhere if you look for it. You see it in the rowing machine you bought yourself thinking that's how you'd tone your body, only now it's where you hang yesterday's and tomorrow's clothes. You never thought it had this function when you bought it, but on bad days it even talks to you, reminding you in a satnav accent that you never manage to follow through on your intentions, that you lack willpower, backbone, spirit.

Or relationships. Aren't many of them just one month of bliss followed by five years wondering when the bliss is coming back again, what happened to the bliss, who hid the bliss? And what about nights out, what about the sesh? How often have you found yourself wanting to leave, finding your coat, miraculously with your phone, wallet and keys still in it, made it to the door, only for a friend to grab you by the shoulder and implore you with eyes that look like they've just witnessed multiple murders, to stay, please stay, for me, please stay.

The sesh is actually a good example of how unsatisfactory life can be. Spending time with friends is a real pleasure, a real joy, but at a certain point the mood changes from the joy of seeing your friends to the fear of going home alone. For many of us there's just never enough. We can't stop wanting. But if we examine the wanting at a micro level we'll see that it's unsatisfactory. It's just wanting for the sake of wanting, and this is how most of us function most of the time. Is it any wonder that cocaine is as popular as it is?

If you're not satisfied now, what makes you think you ever will be? I got asked that question once by a girlfriend in the middle of an argument that would eventually break us up. The argument had come about, as many of them did in that relationship, because I was deeply unhappy. Often when we're unhappy it takes us the longest time to realise that we're the source of that unhappiness, and back then, I was blaming her, the United States of America, the publishing industry, my father and the parking ticket I'd just got because I thought I would be the exception who didn't get caught parked in a loading bay. I made a long list of reasons for my unhappiness that didn't include me. If your long list doesn't include you, it'll take you most of your lifetime to get to the end of it.

'I'm just not satisfied with my life,' I told her, and she followed up with 'If you're not satisfied now, what makes you think you ever will be?'

We were in a café in a hippy town called Ojai, north of Los Angeles. I got up, went to the counter and ordered a lemongrass kombucha.

Many years later, I went back to Ojai, not the actual place but through the writings of Jiddu Krishnamurti, who lived in Ojai for a time. Krishnamurti was a great teacher. He was so good that I've used this quote before. If I could, I mean, if I could get away with it, I'd write a book that had this quote on every page: 'There is great happiness in not wanting, in not being someone, in not going somewhere.' I wouldn't have got that back then. I hadn't quite reached the end of my long list yet. But as soon as I did, as soon as I realised that looking for satisfaction outside yourself, looking for satisfaction from things was impossible, the truth of what Krishnamurti said stopped me in my tracks.

Exercise: Eat the blame

This is a fairly radical teaching from Tibet.

Whenever something bad happens and you're looking for someone to blame for your sense of dissatisfaction, start with yourself.

Of course not all the time, but in many circumstances we can eat some of the blame ourselves, and this is where we can learn.

By recognising that I shouldn't have believed that, or I shouldn't have invested in this, or I should have followed my instinct there, I can learn from my mistakes and actually grow.

It's empowering. But also really difficult. It's uncomfortable when we recognise that we have been blaming other people instead of growing up ourselves.

But ultimately growing up means getting to know ourselves and accept ourselves and be kind to ourselves, blame or no blame.

Emptiness and the Bog of Allen

I am tired. Too full of stuff I've done. Where my legs hurt where my scalp hurts. I'll not fight the thing inside me anymore. Let it eat me up. Please God. I want it to.

— EIMEAR McBRIDE

We are empty, or rather the matter of which we are composed is empty … the world in which we live is part of a flux, a stream of events. This does not mean it is nothing. Everything depends on everything else. Nothing exists on its own. On account of all the influences that come to bear upon them, things appear, exist, and disappear, and then reappear again. But they never exist independently.

— THE DALAI LAMA

Some years ago I came to the end of my tether in the California desert. I'd moved to Los Angeles on the back of a promised book deal. I'd written a dystopian sci-fi thriller about psychedelic water. I had an agent who loved the book, and a film company in Los Angeles wanted to option it. I had a girlfriend and a dog and we were living together at the beach. And on top of all that I'd won a grant from the Swiss government to do research on masculinity. I was, briefly, it seemed, at the peak of my power.

Now any seasoned meditator will tell you that the good times are often harder to navigate than the bad ones. During the tough times, you get it, okay, this is *dukkha*. This is suffering. The goal of meditation is to end suffering, so let's get to work. But in the good times your senses are often numbed by a serene mist of positivity and joy, and you forget to meditate. The good times are a trap. Watch out for the good times. They're banana skins.

When you fall in love you forget to meditate. When you come into a bit of money you forget to meditate. When you wake up with no stress or anxiety, you forget to meditate. Or worse, you assume that you've passed all the important trials, and can now rest easy. Reader, there's no enlightened retirement. Life is a game with no half-time interval, and no time-outs, and no last-minute substitutions. There are no holidays or long weekends. The testing, I mean your testing, never stops. Søren Kierkegaard said 'To be human is not a fact but a task.' I don't think he was wrong.

Less than a year after coming to Los Angeles to live the dream as a writer, I was down to my last couple of hundred dollars and living in the back of my truck in the desert. I couldn't afford to pay rent on my place any more, which was bad enough, but made worse by the fact that the home I couldn't afford was a storage container with no windows, cold water and a redneck septic tank beneath it that made more noise than a pond full of frogs.

I remember stopping for gas one day and a sun-bleached clerk asking me, 'How's life, partner?'

'Life's like a bad country and western song,' I replied. 'I've lost my money, my house, my girl and my dog this week.'

'Well, at least you find out who your people are when you're down on your luck,' he said.

I decided to go home to Kildare. It was summer, so rather than spend my time at my parents' home, I went to work on my grandmother's garden. It wasn't a huge plot. My grandmother lived in a small semi-d in an estate, but her garden was full and it was neglected, and I could have spent a month on my knees and not removed all the weeds. My gran would come out and ask me if I was wearing suncream at least once an hour. In the evenings, I'd drive out to the Bog of Allen and, perched on the warm hood of the car, I'd watch the sun setting across Offaly, Meath and Roscommon. As a young lad growing up, the dream was to get a job working on the bog. You made bank digging brown gold. You got a tan. The old fellas let you smoke fags all day even though you were only fourteen. You learned new curse words. But we never loved the bog. It felt like a hateful, starving place.

A good friend from Allenwood, who fled the place when she was only sixteen, once described it to me in angry language, as if she were talking about an ex. 'It's a nothingness. It's an absence. It's a weight around your ankles.

It's a black pit of despair. People go missing there,' she said, 'They get sucked in and devoured. Why would you even want to, Conor?'

Folks out there would say there's nothing but a sliver of barbed wire between Kildare and Galway, which was unfair. The bog is rich. It's rich with foxes, red squirrels, predatory birds and some of the toughest plants on the planet. The bog isn't a wasteland – unless you were forced to grow up there; it's not nothing; the bog just seems empty compared to the rest of the country. And the bog only seems empty because everywhere else we live in the world is so packed, so cluttered. Being empty is a positive. If you're full, you can't fit any more in, but if you're empty the potential is immense.

Emptiness is a Buddhist concept. This might seem a little nihilistic, but at a cold, theoretical level a lot of Buddhism does look that way. It's only when you live and experience it that you get to see that it's not. Emptiness means that neither you, nor I, nor any other phenomenon in the entire universe is permanent, separate or independent. Nothing is full. Nothing is done. Nothing is ever over. Nothing is finished. Nothing is truly alone. Nothing is separate. This is a very useful thought to play with. It's comforting. Nothing is as big, bad or as important as it seems.

I was once on retreat in the north of Italy. That's something remarkable about retreat spaces – they are as a rule never in ugly parts of the world. I've always been a bad student, and on this retreat it was no different. It was a ten-day retreat, so for ten days, I couldn't talk to anyone, couldn't read a book, couldn't use my phone and could only eat two meals a day. But, like I said, I've always been a bad student, and I've never been good at accepting the rules, even though I knew all about them when I signed up. I hid a book among my belongings. I had granola bars bundled inside my socks. I kept my phone on me, stashed it beneath the insole of my shoe. Not that anyone would have come looking through my belongings. I was caught up in a story: surrendering to the retreat while preserving my comforts, the little things I needed to feel good. This story made it extra hard for me to meditate. I'd find myself sitting in the hall at four in the morning trying to focus on my breath but instead wondering what would happen if the phone turned itself back on and started making ringing noises and everyone found out.

Eventually, on day three, I went to the course teacher and told him that I'd smuggled my phone in and it was killing me, and would he be so kind as to take it back. The course teacher, Davide, was a huge man. I found out later that it was glandular – something had gone haywire inside him, and he'd changed from a skinny little monk into a balloon-shaped giant over a summer. I expected him to throw me out of the course, or to give me a brutal lecture, but instead he was laughing when I came to see him.

'Do you ever cook?' he asked me.

'Yes,' I said.

'Do you ever use a cast-iron skillet?'

'I do.'

'You know how the handle becomes hot as the pan becomes hot?'

'Yes.'

'And what happens when you hold on to the handle?'

'You burn your hand,' I said.

'Everything in the entire universe has the power to burn your hand if you hold on to it,' he said. 'Everything is constantly changing. It's neither here nor there, it's empty. So don't hold on. It's only empty. Let it go.'

I gave him my phone and my book. I kept the granola bars, though. Change for me has always been two steps forward and one step back.

But back to the bog. Here's the thing: if you stare into the bog, the bog will eventually stare into you. Those evenings, driving across the bog in my mother's boxy Citroën Picasso and staring deep into it was my simple way of working through an identity crisis, of understanding my own emptiness. I'd gone from being a bright new writing talent in Los Angeles, fielding calls from agents, bragging at pool parties to a guy in his thirties sleeping on his parents' sofa, sitting at their dinner table, fielding questions like whether I'd have the ice cream or some yoghurt or both over the roar of a too-big television screen and *Gogglebox*.

Inviting emptiness is a great relief when you've spent so much of your life caught up in your identity. I have a student in her fifties. When she was sixteen she was hit by a car and broke her leg in half a dozen places. It took her an entire summer to heal. As you get older, summers aren't that long, but when you're a teenager they can be interminable, especially when everyone you know is out falling in love and getting drunk for the first time. That injury really did a number on her, and so she did a peculiar thing that maybe many of us humans do: she decided to never heal.

Her leg began functioning again but she decided to act like she was still lame. For forty years she's treated her perfectly fine, perfectly working leg as if it were made of bone china. She'd reply to all hiking or jogging invites with, 'I'd better check in on the leg first.' She stuck to her story like a getaway driver under police interrogation.

Sticking to your story is great when you're up against a good cop/bad cop routine, but it's a pathway to misery when you're not. The way to travel through life is not to stick but to flow. From one instant to the next, from one dramatic change to the next, if we can remember the lesson of emptiness, we won't get caught up in limiting beliefs, we won't get stuck, we won't become frozen.

Early dial-up internet in Kildare was a lesson in patience, frozen screens and knowing when to wait and when to press reset. The Bog of Allen is a type of geographical reset. It's a five-county-wide reflection hunkered between the Liffey and the Shannon. Back in the day, folks used to call it the Bog of Jobby. Jobby was a giant and the bog, they said, was his toilet. When I was growing up, if you said 'toilet' it meant you were posh. If you called the bathroom 'the bog', you were local.

On one of my road trips into the bog I stopped and spoke to a guy of about my age who'd given up a job in Canada to come home and run the Bog of Allen interpretive centre.

'Do tourists actually come here?'

'School trips mostly. It's no Glendalough, though. The bog is a hard sell. Come out and feel the wind.'

We walked out across the bog along a trail made of railway sleepers until we were beyond the trees and the wind was whipping against us like wet towels. We ducked inside a small hut.

'It's not a wasteland,' he said, 'the bog is full of old roads, buried treasures, mysteries, but yeah, with all that wind, it's a hard sell.'

Meditation's a hard sell too. It goes against society's insistence that we should be always wanting something, always striving. We long to attach significance and importance to everything we do. We cling to our past pain, and we chase relentlessly after future success, forgetting that it's also okay to be happy now. And meditation is hard. The reward is buried treasure. The treasure is when we recognise emptiness as future potential and then set ourselves free from our past, and from all our stories.

Exercise: Emptiness

Emptiness is hard to explain. It's better understood if you can feel it. It happens when we see through all the fixed notions that we have of ourselves. A simple, but not always easy, way to do this is to observe feelings and thoughts as they arise.

Sit down comfortably.

Take a few deep breaths.

Wait for your breath to return to normal and then bring your attention to its rhythm.

Follow the rhythm.

When a thought appears, and it should pretty quickly, just observe that thought without becoming involved in it. Observe it like it's somebody else's thought and not your own.

If you do this, and you manage to not become involved in the thought – and believe me, this is often as tricky as spotting a typo on Twitter and not telling the world about it – you'll see that the thought gradually fades.

The thought is inherently empty.

The more often you can bring yourself to this realisation, the clearer it becomes for you.

Many of the great meditation teachers in this world come from Tibet. Tibet is famous for its vast open spaces, and no doubt some people who grow up there think of them as nothing, or empty.

Kalu Rinpoche, a Tibetan teacher, who to the best of my knowledge never visited the Bog of Allen, at least not in the flesh, said it like this: 'We live in illusion and the appearance of things. There is a reality. We are that reality. When you understand this, you see that you are nothing, and being nothing, you are everything. That is all.'

Sure Look

May misfortune follow you the rest of your life, but never catch up.

— IRISH PROVERB

If you have a problem that can be fixed, then there is no use in worrying. If you have a problem that cannot be fixed, then there is no use in worrying.

— BUDDHIST PROVERB

My parents taught me a lot about perspective, but it took me an incredibly long time to learn the lesson. They had a way of looking at things that allowed them to ride more smoothly over the inevitable bumps and breakdowns of the life they'd chosen. We often couldn't afford things. We had no TV, we had no shower, the one bicycle I remember getting as a kid was so big for me I had to walk it around the place like a dog on a lead until my bones grew. At one stage I remember us having two cars but neither of them worked. They sat outside the front of our house, rusted sides, soft tyres, windows that if you opened you couldn't close again.

Once or twice a year, my dad would manage to get one of the cars running for long enough to attempt the drive north to my grandparents and cousins in Belfast. My sister and I would argue about which side of the back seat we'd sit on. It was an argument I always lost, and on wet days this meant getting wet feet from the rainwater leaking through the chassis.

Modern cars have a lot more cohesion about them, but back then something was always flying off the side or from under our car as we sped along. It was as if leaving Kildare had the same mechanical force on our bangers as re-entering the atmosphere has on rockets. My father was pretty good in these situations. While my mother, my sister and I (and our dog, Kerry, a highly intuitive Dalmatian who in hindsight was the glue that held our family together) stayed in the car saying prayers, he'd run off and come back with the spare tyre, the oil filter or the length of twine needed to get the car moving again. My dad never panicked in emergencies. In a way, I think he kinda liked them. Whenever he found himself with his back against the wall, something peaceful opened up in him, as if he were thinking to himself, 'Yes, life, you're finally happening.'

Some folks are like that. I worked with a mad chef out in the Hamptons who dipped into an angelic serenity on Saturday evenings, with one hundred reservations, two waiters missing in action and a brown-out in the kitchen.

'We're fucked,' he'd say and start laughing to himself. It was the only time you ever saw him not frowning. I have another friend who seems happiest when he's being evicted, fired or dumped. Drama brings him to life. He loves the beginnings and the endings of relationships. It's the middle part that kills him.

My dad was one of these men. The middle parts killed him too. In what you might call a perverse way, the more the world around my father disintegrated, the more he took on the look of a guy alone in a bubble bath enjoying his own farts. When everyone else was losing their heads, he suddenly found his. My dad: only use in emergencies. Panic set in at all other times, especially in the living room at a minute past six, when we'd turned each cushion inside out, set the dog on the scent, emptied all our pockets and still couldn't find the remote control to turn on the news.

Our homes were inherently unstable structures too. Mutiny was never far away. I can remember one time a goat that had escaped from the slaughterhouse up the road tried to jump through our living room window. The window was closed and the animal bounced back onto the street. One winter a back boiler leaked through the wall and the hallway was suddenly ankle-deep in cold brown water. Our chimney caught fire each autumn. We'd run out of the house and cross the street, and watch beneath blankets as tiny tongues of fire shot out of the twin stacks. 'Sure look,' my dad would say, taking papers and tobacco out of his shirt pocket and building a smoke, 'it was always going to happen.'

There's something about the expression 'sure look'. Something about its capacity to mean nothing yet explain everything at the same time. It's a way of invoking a higher power, an admission that there's nothing more that could have been done. It's in god's lap now kinda thing. It rained for a solid month, the horse dropped dead in the night, the star fell out of the sky, the money got spent, but sure look.

It works the opposite way too. It can also invoke the lowest power around, that of the perpetual fuck-up. It's a way of turning the blame back on the accuser: What did you expect? Why was I given the responsibility anyway? Don't you know I'm just some useless eejit, and now you only have yourself to blame for thinking it'd be any different.

Many years later, I brought a girlfriend home to visit. She was from Canada and was studying in Dublin, and I should have known that she wasn't going to stick around, but yeah, that's why you try to get in the hard lessons young. I was pretty insecure around her, on account of the fact that she was beautiful, and educated and wealthy, and I was just a bartender who she'd slipped her number to.

That night, after dinner with my parents, we went to the local pub, just me and her. We hadn't planned on getting drunk, but I suppose the tension of her meeting my folks needed to go somewhere, and I was a long way from sitting with my breath at that stage. There was a guy in the bar doing Neil Diamond covers with a guitar and a drum machine. We stayed out till two and heard 'Sweet Caroline' three times, oh, oh oh.

The next morning, my dad knocked on our room door. 'Did you take the car anywhere?' he asked. At this stage, my family had moved up in the world, and we now had two fully working cars outside our home. We even had a new home. Two showers. TVs as big as windows. Romantica instead of Viennetta.

'I didn't,' I said.

'Strange. It's gone, and so are the keys. Did you lock the front door when you came home last night?'

'I can't remember, possibly no.'

'Ah, see, it was open this morning.'

'Do you think the car was stolen?'

'I think so.'

'Shit, sorry.'

'Sure look, nothing can be done now.'

I know my parents always over-performed when my sister or I brought partners back. They had a bit of the cattle trader to them – Let's not ruin a potential sale by saying too much.

Months later, after a rush of blood to the head, I made my way to Vancouver in the middle of January, and watched as that girlfriend's ex-boyfriend made moves to win her back on ski hills, while I floundered in snowdrifts with chapped lips and ice down my pants. She was never really that into me, but I do remember that day when my dad's car was stolen and how she looked at me, and with a gormless expression that jarred with the very expensive, elite education she'd had, said, 'Your parents are so chill.'

There is a famous old Zen story of a farmer in Japan. This guy had a horse, but one day his horse ran away. All the neighbours gathered round when they saw his horse was gone, and said, 'Oh, you poor man, you're so unlucky, life has been so horrible for you.' And the farmer responded, 'Maybe.' The next day the farmer's horse returned, and it brought with it two other wild horses. Again, all the neighbours gathered round, only this time they said, 'Such a lucky man, you've been so blessed.' And the farmer responded, 'Maybe.' Two days later, the farmer's son tried to ride one of the wild horses and he fell off, breaking his leg badly. Guess what, the neighbours gathered round again and started lamenting, 'Oh, you poor man, just look at your life,' etc. – you're getting the picture – and guess what, the farmer responded: 'Maybe.' And then the next day – it really was an eventful week – the local military arrived in the village and they enlisted every young man in the village and sent them off to the war. All of them except for the farmer's son, whose leg was busted. The neighbours gathered round and said, 'You're so lucky.' And the farmer simply said, 'Maybe.'

Two days after my dad's car was stolen, he received a call from the guards. 'We've located your car, Mr Creighton, if you'd like to come along and identify it. We don't believe there's been any damage to the vehicle.' When my dad brought the car home, he opened the boot and found a flatscreen TV.

'We should give it back,' my mother said.

'Ah, sure look it, it's here now,' my dad said.

In Zen we talk about a thing called the discriminating mind. Our minds are constantly judging, deciding if something is good or bad. In fact, if you examine your thoughts you'll see that they invariably fall into four categories: wanting, remembering, planning and judging. Judging is simply our mind's way of managing the world around us. But judgement closes us off to things. Judgement tells us I like this, but I don't like that. I like her, but I don't like him.

Shunryu Suzuki, a serious black belt in the world of meditation, said, 'In the beginner's mind there are many possibilities; in the expert's mind there are few.' The discriminating mind is a useful tool. It tells us when something is safe, or when it might be dangerous. But if it becomes too dominant, then we'll confuse it with our own identity. The trick is to suspend judgement; to adopt a 'don't know' mind; to treat all situations like you're a beginner, like you're new to them. My dad had it naturally. When something happened, he never rushed to label it good or bad. His response was simply, 'Is that so?' Now Zen would never encourage you to consider keeping property that wasn't yours, especially not an expensive plasma TV. That's very much my dad's attitude. Even if the TV did eventually go back, his attitude would be to wait and see, to observe without judgement.

In the Zen tradition, there are many poems called koans. They are short statements, really, meant to provoke the mind, inspire a sudden shift in perspective. Here's one I just made:

> What harm
> You never know
> We'll see
> Sure look

Exercise: Non-judgement

Only with an open attitude and without any prejudice is it possible to really perceive what is present in our lives. Each judgement distorts the image by putting a filter over it. That sounds understandable and simple: Without a filter, the image is pure and genuine, just as it is.

But we constantly evaluate. Our brain is judging always and everywhere: it criticises, praises and evaluates. This is normal, this is how our brain works. In ancient times this judging and evaluating brain helped us survive in a constantly dangerous and insecure world. Judging everything simply means that we are human and have a human brain.

Being mindful does not ask us to stop this judgment, because this would simply not be possible. Mindfulness, however, teaches us to notice our constant tendency to judge and then consciously free ourselves from it. This creates a choice as to whether we want to believe our inner – judging – voice or recognise that 'This is a thought. This is judging.' The more we practise non-judgement, the more open and free we become, the more we let things and people be as they actually are: without filter, without category, just the pure being.

Practising this non-judging can be an extremely reward-ing and exciting activity. We will probably switch into automatic pilot again and again, forgetting this higher level of awareness that allows us to observe ourselves think. However, with some practice – and a lot of patience and gentleness when we wander off again – we may catch ourselves more and more in our daily judging of people and situations. This can be a very liberating and enlightening process which will bring us a little closer to reality each time.

Set a timer for five minutes.

On a sheet of paper beside you, write down up to five of the big subjects in your life: your job, your parents, your partner (or best friend), yourself. You could write it down like this:

> meditation teacher
> Ray and Siobhan
> Conor

Close your eyes and begin by focusing on your breath. And then slowly move from one subject to the next and observe the judgements that arise. Don't become attached to the judgements, and certainly don't believe them; just watch them and see what your judging mind gets up to. The more you understand how the mechanics of your brain work, the more you can demystify the process, and the more you can observe your thoughts free from judgement, the greater freedom will be yours.

What RIP.ie can Teach Us about Life

Her past is behind her, her future is of little concern. She moves towards the grave, at her own speed.

— ANNE ENRIGHT

People go through life blindly, ignoring death like revellers at a party feasting on fine foods. They ignore that later they will have to go to the toilet, so they do not bother to find out where there is one. When nature finally calls, they have no idea where to go and are in a mess.

— AJAHN CHAH

If I can credit my upbringing with anything, it was the relentless exposure to death. Our home was midway between two great institutions of eternal rest: the chapel and the slaughterhouse. Depending on the day, the bells drowned out the cattle's lowing or the lowing drowned out the bells.

One of my first sources of income was working funerals as an altar boy. For some reason, they paid best, better than baptisms and weddings, supposedly the happiest day of people's lives. A funeral could get you a tenner. Sometimes more. At a wedding, you got a fiver in an envelope. At a funeral, they just transferred whatever was in their pocket into yours. No ceremony.

Three deaths stand out from the first twenty years of my life: my granddad Alex, my dog Kerry and my best friend Kevin. Each one brought with it its own sense of tragedy. Each one set in motion its own series of events, and each one taught me a new and important lesson about life.

Alex, my granddad on my mum's side, died when I was about twelve. He was a jazz musician, or at least had been back in the day, before he'd fathered five children and had to hang up his saxophone and go to work behind a bar. His funeral was not a homage to the many years he'd spent rolling kegs and bouncing drunks; it was a tribute to music. My family rented a ballroom. Alex's body was placed in the middle, in an open casket, wearing a blue suit with a bright handkerchief in the breast pocket, his hair slicked back towards his ears. And all around him, people I'd never met, men who were not part of my family, but who all had that same never-settling-down, shirt-tails-untucked, three-day-growth style about them, took turns playing their horns and ukuleles in the direction of the body, and then swapping with other musicians to go and take their place at the bar. They'd ruffle my hair on the way past.

'What are you having, John?' (a decent guess at a kid's name, to be fair), they'd ask.

'A Cidona,' I'd say.

'Not today, John. Today you can have a real drink.'

My granddad's funeral was the first time in my life I got drunk. It did not take much. A small Guinness with blackcurrant. For me it was like an out-of-body experience. For the first time in my life I understood what it was like to operate from a place of no fear. I can remember approaching the coffin and placing my hand inside, and then running my hand along the length of my dead granddad's sleeve until I found his skin and pinched it. That was death and I touched it.

That same year, I went away for the summer to the Gaeltacht, and when I came back my mum had had our dog, Kerry, put down. The strange thing is, I can't even remember her being that old. Stranger still, I have a number of friends who had their family dogs euthanised when they were away in the Gaeltacht. All of them say the same thing: I don't think she was so old that my mum needed to do that.

Kerry had been a constant figure in my life. My first therapist. I told her everything. The gentlest Dalmatian, with eyes that said, 'I see you, I hear you, you're safe.' When Kerry died, I felt more alone in that house then I'd ever been before.

We got a couple more dogs but there was no replacing Kerry. One was a deaf mongrel called Pax, who had a habit of getting out the back door and running into traffic. She didn't last long. Jenny came along somewhat later. My sister named that one. She was a purebred Dalmatian, like Kerry, but she would not be trained. She made a mockery of Kerry's legacy. She wouldn't walk on the leash. She never responded to her name. She tore shoes asunder at the ripe old age of four, and my mother had her put down before she was even eight.

My grandfather's death was the end of my childhood; Kerry's death was the beginning of my life as a teenager; but Kevin's death was the end of my life in Ireland.

Kevin was a punk from Navan and he was so far ahead of his time that if he was still alive today, we wouldn't have caught up with him. He ate no meat. He cared about CO_2 emissions. He hated homophobia. He listened when you spoke, and unlike nearly every single other lad I grew up with in the nineties, he never once made a 'That's what she said' joke.

Kevin had a short green mohawk and a safety pin through his ear. On the back of his denim jacket, he had an iron-on patch that read DISCRIMINATION HURTS. When he was only nineteen, he tied his arms and legs together and threw himself over the quay wall and into the Liffey. Just the previous day, we'd been sitting in a bar on Suffolk Street discussing our mental health, and Kevin had mentioned being depressed.

'I've got the blues,' he said.

'Would you not talk to someone?', I said.

'Like a head doctor?'

'Yeah.'

'Sure, I'm too fucked for that carry-on.'

'Yeah. Fair enough.'

Welcome to real talk in nineties Ireland. We had no language to express things, and no tools to unlock our problems. I was depressed, too. I didn't know many young men of my age who weren't. I had no experience or training in how to talk to the suicidal. Lo and behold, the following morning Kevin killed himself. At the funeral, there was an open casket, but I didn't look. News had filtered back from those ahead of me in the line that the undertakers had combed his mohawk out and removed the safety pin from his ear. 'It doesn't look like him any more,' they said. 'I don't want to look,' I said. 'Sometimes it's better to remember them as they were.'

Kevin's death was a little like the beginning of my life. Or at least my deliberate life. Up until that point, I'd let things happen to me. I'd allowed my parents to happen to me, Kildare to happen to me, the long years of cycling headlong into horizontal rain, skidding across the bog, happen to me. But when Kevin's death happened, I decided, as Henry David Thoreau decided when he moved out into the woods, albeit within walking distance of his momma's cooking, to live deliberately. I left Ireland and moved to Italy, and I kept moving. I was a bit of a mess. I loved wine and arguing. I loved drugs for a while too. I lived in squats, palaces and bizarre room shares in Berlin. I went to war zones. I almost died on more than a few occasions. Through it all, I felt flickers of happiness but was mostly miserable, and eventually this brought me to meditation, and to India, and back to death.

'When we don't understand death, life can be very confusing,' the great teacher Ajahn Chah said.

I remember living at a monastery in the Himalayas. I was quite new to meditation at this stage, but I was cocky. I think this is pretty common in novice meditators. You have a couple of insights, you see some flashing lights, feel some mild psychedelic current shoot through your spine and suddenly you convince yourself that you're the next incarnation of Buddha. The head monk was a little man with rotten teeth. His job was to make sure I was okay, and to generally keep me out of trouble. Westerners were always joining Indian monasteries, and then going nuts.

He came over to where I was sitting on my cushion and said, 'Tonight is a very special night. Tonight we're going to meditate on death.' One of the monks had died recently. They took his body and laid it at the base of a *stupa* – the tiny tombs dotted around the monastery – and then covered it in flowers and candles. And all night along, wrapped in blankets and sitting cross-legged, we made a circle around the body and meditated on death. It was fairly normal for us to do late-night meditation vigils. Sometime after midnight, or two in the morning, the head monk would decide enough was enough, and we could all go to bed, but that night when we meditated on death, we stayed there till the sun had risen, the monkeys were zipping past our heads, and the building crew were already splitting rocks to make a footpath lower down the valley. It was exhausting and it knocked the bluster out of me.

The next day the head monk came to speak to me after lunch. 'How was it?', he asked. 'I'm still tired,' I said. 'Good,' he replied. 'I hope you're always tired so you can understand the importance of thinking about death. If death comes to you today, you'll be ready.'

A lot of Buddhist effort is in preparation for death. The long hours of meditation are a type of clearing-away project. The more junk you can shovel from your mind, the less you're going to have to wade through when you finally kick the bucket. Whenever the head monk saw me after morning chanting, he'd always come over and say, 'Great, you're alive another day. You can get so much more work done. Don't waste a second.'

How many times have you heard the expression, 'You'll catch your death'? As a kid, it felt like the standard thing that grown-ups shouted at us, any day the temperature was less than 12 degrees. Every time you ran out to play, someone had to remind you of what might be lurking out there. Death was always close at hand. Local news was basically this: 'Do you know such and such, she went to school with so and so, you do, you do, she had the shop up town, well she's dead now. Died two weeks ago. In her sleep. Shocking.' Maybe it's because we're an island community, or maybe it's because we do actually know everyone here, but each trip down the country for me always involved a listing of those who had passed. 'But I don't even know these people,' I'd say. 'Oh but you do, you do, you have to,' came the reply, as if to say, it doesn't matter that you don't know who the deceased was, the important thing is on this planet, on this day, another person died.

We have a much closer relationship with death than our European cousins. While the traditional wake has been consigned to the fringes of the island, and the islands off the island, most people will still have seen an open casket at some stage in their life. We've all seen dead people. And especially if you grew up in the country, on trips home you'll notice that if your parents are not in watching TV in the evening, they're at a removal, a funeral, a month's mind. RIP.ie gets more traffic than the weather. There are laundry businesses who survive by doing funeral suits. We talk about death a lot in Ireland, though we rarely contemplate it. But it's actually through the contemplation of death that life shows us its true meaning.

'Meditating on death could make us a lot happier,' says meditation teacher Sharon Salzberg, 'We can feel free from so many of life's irritations and annoyances and be truly in awe of the miracle of life and the time we do have. If we deeply see the folly of holding on, we can be much more in harmony with the flow of change.'

Exercise: On death

It can be a very beautiful practice to imagine that each morning you wake up, you've been given an extra day of life. Leave a note by your bedside with the simple phrase: ONE MORE DAY.

Another exercise is to imagine that you're meeting everyone for the last time. This can be especially good if you have to go home to your family and you're worried about getting triggered by old feelings. Just think, and it's not such a wild thing to think, that everyone at the table might be dead in a day, a week, a year. This could be your very last conversation. Are you sure you want to end it on a sour note?

Another way you can integrate death into life is to meditate on how much time you have left to live. Write down some figures on a piece of paper and then set a timer. From time to time, open your eyes and gaze at the paper beside you. It can say something like:

> two weeks
> six months
> five years

Try to fully embody the experience and dive into the feeling of only having a certain, short amount of time to live. Does this change your perspective? Might it influence your decision to hold on to grudges, or to continue with certain projects?

Losing the Head

Grief is being angry that the sun is still shimmering away, smiling in the sky.

— SINÉAD GLEESON

Racism is a heart disease that's curable.

— RUTH KING

It's very easy to watch the news and feel angry. It's very easy
to fall into an innocuous conversation with a friend and find
that somehow you've stumbled on a subject that's making
you or them angry. It happens all the time in relationships.
It happens behind the wheel of car. I used to be an angry
driver. I'd beep and swerve and drive right up behind other
cars. Nowadays I drive a very old Volkswagen van that is
always the slowest thing on the road, so even if I wanted to
drive aggressively I couldn't. I was also an angry footballer.
I once tackled a friend, scythed him down and sent him
rolling off the field. It came out of nowhere and I felt like a
monster. 'It's just a game,' he said from the ground. He was
right. He still is. I decided to quit playing football after that.

Of all the many challenges we are given on our assignment on planet Earth – parallel parking, eating doughnuts without dribbling jam, unlearning the habit of biting our nails, falling asleep at night, and believing in love when our heart's been broken – dealing with anger is one of the hardest.

Anger is what happens when we're confronted with fear or sadness or frustration. It's also, often, a delusion. If we're honest with ourselves, we're not always angry when we feel angry, we're just tired or upset or feeling misunderstood. It's very easy to feel misunderstood these days. The society we've created is inherently unfair, and this, no matter how much we try to inoculate ourselves with objects and excitement, hurts. You know the expression 'You don't hate Mondays, you hate capitalism'?

We often feel angry when we feel we have been wrong. Being wrong produces a pain inside us that's often worse than being wronged because it involves the collapse of our identity. You see it in children all the time. They find a toy on the street and assume it's theirs. But then another parent comes along and asks for it back, and of course you give it back, not to do so would mean you're Satan. And your child starts crying because their identity, which just a second ago included a bright plastic ball, has collapsed.

When your identity collapses as an adult, it can also be an occasion to cry, but I'd urge you, if you ever see an opportunity to take a wrecking ball to your carefully constructed identity, just do it. There are moments – a death, a break-up, a pandemic, you know what I'm talking about – when the things we have built tumble, and in these moments, if we are paying attention, we get glimpses into the nature of reality, and the illusion of the reality we create. When you observe anger, and the safest way to do this is to observe it in yourself, you'll notice that beneath the initial outrage, anger's engine is powered by sadness. Anger is what we do when nobody notices how sad we are.

I grew up in the shadow of an angry man. My dad had a temper. It's hard to remember because he's as gentle as a basket of wool now. But there were times growing up when you could be sent to your room for the tiniest of infractions. There were certain situations where it was best to just hold your breath: at the dinner table, during the news and in the back seat of the car. Our parents programme us, and still today when I hear the opening jingle for the RTÉ news I'll instinctively stop talking. And if I'm a passenger in your car I won't touch the radio, make loud noises or even, however hot I am, roll my window down.

My dad was angry because his reality wasn't how he wanted it to be. I'll bet you my collection of spiritual books with blue and white, sunrise and sunset covers that if you ask anyone why they're angry, they'll tell you it's because their reality is not how they want it to be. I can understand why my dad was angry. He grew up in Belfast during the Troubles. He read *Lord of the Rings*. He listened to *Tubular Bells*. He dreamed of driving a Citroën from Belfast to India. He climbed mountains. He wore Adidas Gazelles. He imagined himself in the Rolling Stones, on the Isle of Wight, a beat poet, a scenester, when he was just a working-class lad from West Belfast. My dad was a romantic. I inherited this. And he was a dreamer, which I also inherited, but he somehow ended up married and the father of two children in a tiny village in Kildare where he was the only Loyalist for two hundred miles, and living off the dole. He was in his twenties. I don't blame him for being angry.

Anger is a test: do you stick out your tongue or do you open your heart? As meditators we're not interested in being right; we only care about being compassionate. All around us people are losing their heads. If you ask me, they'll be at this for a while yet. And when it's safe, when the most important thing is not to duck for cover or leave the room, we can use this anger as a way of exercising our compassion.

My dad got angry last Christmas. I often notice myself getting angry at Christmas too. It's the rawest time of the year. He was angry because I'd been in Dublin with a friend who was spending Christmas alone and decided at the last minute to stay with her rather than come home. It was one of those decisions that I didn't think through. I wasn't practising awareness. Christmas is possibly the least aware time of the year. For me anyway. It's not your family, it's not the weather; the holiday itself is triggering. In the moment it felt right to not go home, so I made my decision. My dad got angry on the phone. 'It's Christmas,' he said, appealing to the occasion. I felt anger rise in me. Wasn't it already a type of miracle that we were talking on the phone, that I was home in the country at all, that the possibility of us sharing food together still existed?

And this is where you get to choose. This is where you either fail or pass the test. Alongside the anger, if you're careful, if you can be with your breath, you'll notice there's understanding, and the more attention you give the understanding the more compassion you can generate. Compassion is like a balm for anger. Try it. Try telling the people who are angry with you that you understand them and that you love them. Maybe they won't listen. Some anger runs very deep. But they'll still hear.

Anyway, in this instance I didn't choose balm, I chose fire. Ram Dass, the spiritual teacher, had a good line: 'If you think you're enlightened, go spend a week with your family.' That evening I came home and the house was empty. I called my mother and she told me she was at A&E. My dad had broken a tendon in his hand opening a bottle of cider. No, he hadn't gone back to drink because I'd upset him, he was just trying to follow a boiled ham and cider recipe and the bottle had slipped in his hand and cut him. When they got back we ate together. Everything had to be microwaved. It tasted dry, like hospital food. My dad was still sad. I said sorry a few times.

We often find ourselves in uncomfortable conversations. We find ourselves face to face with someone who has lost their head. We find ourselves confronted by sadness. We realise that we've been wrong, we've been the bad son. Nobody wants to be the bad son. So much conflict comes when people won't admit to being wrong; they don't want to be with that uncomfortable feeling. But we're meditating, so we can tolerate discomfort for just long enough so that we can learn from it. Emotional discomfort as an adult is just like the growing pains in a teenager's legs.

Anger is one of the most useful things we encounter on this journey. If we investigate it, if we really follow it home, it will lead us to the parts of us that we never go to, the parts of us that we didn't know were there. Anger can lead us to the parts of ourselves that haven't been willing to except that another person has an opinion or a point of view that is different from ours. If you can do this, something magical happens – you connect. Some people don't even get to connect once in a lifetime. But it's our purpose, and when you do it, you know it. When we are present, we can sit through discomfort and not turn away.

Anger is also the fuel that keeps racism running on this planet. As James Baldwin wrote, 'I imagine the reason people cling to their hates so stubbornly is because they sense, once hate is gone, they will be forced to deal with pain.'

Exercise: Sitting with anger

Anger is no different from any of the other strong emotions. It's overwhelming. Learning to sit with any emotion is probably the hardest thing we get tasked with doing as a human. Emotions are like giant waves at sea, and it's much easier to just run away from them. Easier in the short term, perhaps.

Sit down and imagine anger. Bring it to your mind. And then just watch where that anger exists in your body. Is it in your chest, your hands, your stomach? Observe the physical sensations that anger creates and keep observing. Don't dive into the thoughts, just keep your focus on the actual bodily sensations that anger produces. In this way we're not under anger's control, we're exploring anger.

As you explore anger, you'll notice that it's much less powerful than we imagined in the first place. As we explore anger, we'll see its nuances. It's often tinged with sadness. When we recognise sadness in ourselves, we're offered a wonderful opportunity for healing.

What can you say to assuage the sadness right now?

What can you say to yourself to make it better?

The Craic

A laugh is a terrible weapon.

— KATE O'BRIEN

A talent for speaking differently, rather than for arguing well, is the chief instrument of cultural change.

— RICHARD RORTY

Don't just do something, sit there.

Ba-dum-ch! That's a meditation joke. We're not exactly known for our comedy. There aren't many jokes in this world, and when they come they're all on you. But as you get deeper into the practice you begin to understand how important humour is. The humour comes from recognising, over and over and over again, that the thing you were looking for was right in front of you the whole time, or that the thing that was causing you pain was your own fingers pinching your leg. The humour arises when you recognise how you're the chief cause of your suffering. When you see that once again, like all the other times before, so much of what you're feeling is on account of you.

As humans, one thing is certain: we will know a lot of pain. That can't be avoided. The original story of the Buddha is that he grew up in a palace where his father tried to shield him from death, sickness and poverty. When the Buddha discovered suffering existed, he committed his life to discovering and eradicating its causes. This meant that he tried to end, not death or sickness or poverty, but the extra suffering that accompanies them. We suffer when we personalise pain. Cancer strikes and we think why me? Your lover leaves and you think you're the unluckiest person in the world. Someone dies young and we say they were taken too young, but who's to say when a person should or shouldn't go?

We all live in a type of auto-pilot state. We're all victims of our own biases. You might grow up supporting your county. You don't know why, you just do, even though you don't even like their colours. You meet one of the players and he's rude to you, but your allegiance remains unbroken. Someone talks shit about your home town, something you do yourself all the time, but now it's someone else, so you fight back. We support our biases like we support our counties. We feed our views. We look for fuel for our opinions. We read the news we agree with. We don't like the friends who call us out, or the ones who say,

'Well, it takes two people to be in a relationship – was she really as bad as you're making her out to be?'

We all have our own stories. We cling to them to our detriment, because they are often incomplete or wrong.

'Don't date people who have nothing but bad things to say about their exes.' A woman from Athy called Posie told me that once in the Lily O'Brien's workers' canteen. She must have been sixty; I was eighteen and the only man working there. It was assembly line work; the chocolates came racing along a type of giant shopping belt and we had to put them into boxes. The other women gave me a hard time because I really wasn't very good at it. One day Posie joined me for lunch and asked me why I was there. 'I need the money,' I said. 'You don't,' she said, 'you need to believe in yourself.' Posie gave me three pieces of advice during that lunch break:

'Don't have expectations.'

'Assume everyone you meet is struggling, and that's the reason they act the way they do.'

'Don't date people who have nothing but bad things to say about their exes. These people can't see their blind spots.'

Blind spots are dangerous. When we have fixed views of ourselves, we're limited and we miss out on so much potential for growth. In meditation, when we stumble on a blind spot, or when we realise we've been wrong, we get the chance to do something very cathartic and healing: laugh at ourselves.

I once made a complete ass of myself working in a bar in Dublin. When you've been a bartender for a while you develop a bias. You become prickly. You can sense bad behaviour almost everywhere. Your bias for rudeness becomes so extreme that if someone doesn't bookend their order with a 'Would you mind awfully …?' and an 'I'm eternally in your gratitude', you assume they're a hateful brute. Not all bartenders become this way, but anyone who deals with drunks – taxi drivers, bouncers, A&E nurses – knows that it requires the kind of patience that our human brains don't really come equipped with.

One night this guy who was seated at a table close to the bar shouted his order up at me, and I responded in the most solidly presumptive way ever by shouting back, 'Are your legs broken or something?' They weren't broken, they were worse than broken – they weren't even there. The guy was in a wheelchair. He was an amputee. Needless to say, he and his friends didn't pay for another drink all night.

We seem to have some idea of ourselves that we must get things right, that to be wrong is to be somehow less human. The problem with that is it screws us because it creates a desire to always be right. It's so important to get used to being wrong and even to look at it with some humour.

Some of us – and yes, I've been this guy too – get so addicted to being right that we find it hard to be in a relationship with others who might point out that we're wrong. If you find it hard to be told you're wrong from time to time, you'll probably find it easiest to be single. But, single or not, you're also in a relationship with yourself. And just as when you discover unexpected text messages on your partner's phone, or find a box of cigarettes in a coat pocket when they said they'd quit five years ago, as you sit in silence you will almost certainly learn uncomfortable things about yourself. At moments like these, it pays not to take yourself too seriously.

Allen Ginsberg had an idea of what I'm talking about. He called it the 'surprise mind'. We really don't know what's going to come up in our heads next, so why take it so personally? Reacting or not reacting is a choice, but as for what comes up, no, there's no choice there. Our mind is a lot like a flea market. Occasionally you find a vintage lampshade for a fiver, but mostly you're just sifting through damp, wool-mix, moth-stripped geansaís from St Bernard.

My granddad used to fart all the way through Sunday lunch. He'd been a jazz musician when he was younger, as

I've mentioned, and as he got older and his colon loosened, he just played his music through his butt. We loved him for it, and I think the reason we did is that he didn't take it personally. We'd sit there eating mashed potato with white pepper and butter, Yorkshire puddings that tasted like doughnuts dipped in gravy, and chicken that was so juicy it breaks my heart that I don't eat meat today. And each time my granddad would let rip, he'd say, 'Ooh, mushy peas,' and laugh about it. In the end he died of colon cancer. That part of him also turned to mush.

When you notice you've been wrong, when you've been at fault, when you've been ignorant and when you've been blind, you get the choice to double down on your opinion or just say, 'Ooh, mushy peas.' We also have the choice of taking ourselves seriously or finding the humour in being human.

This is the humour in meditation. But it's hard won. You only get to laugh after you've spent many a night in tears. Waking up in the spiritual sense is like that scene in *The Truman Show* where Truman reaches the edge of the sea and finds a wall. Don't we all feel that way sometimes? Don't we all walk around with the suspicion that perhaps we're surrounded by actors, or that we too have just been following a type of script?

Meditation can feel like a grim duty. It can be heavy, and it is a lot like performing surgery on ourselves, but when your meditation does become heavy and laborious, you might have made the mistake of thinking you're supposed to be getting somewhere, instead of just being. This simply being is a great balm. We can be with sadness and death and loss and injustice and still feel pain, but not suffer. We can be with the darkest, nastiest sides of ourselves and laugh about it if we want to. Think about it: you didn't decide where to be born, you didn't pick your parents, you don't even get to decide what thoughts co-exist in your brain, so why would you give yourself such a hard time about the parts of you that are often wrong?

When I was in my twenties I attended a friend's funeral in Galway. It was a little like a festival, or even a wedding. It was ridiculous. All my Dublin friends had travelled west for the day. Some of them were close, some were just people you'd stop and chat with; there was even an ex of mine there but she was now dating the guy who used to be her roommate. Sigh. And here we all were, clean, neat, dreadlocks tied back, bondage chains tucked in, spliffs smoked respectfully at a distance from the church, transplanted to the country for a funeral. Justin Timberlake had just gone solo. His song 'Rock Your Body' was everywhere.

You couldn't buy a bottle of Lucozade or a pair of socks without hearing it playing. The church was packed. Half of the congregation were our friends – punks, ravers, potheads – and the other half were friends of his family, proud country folk in slacks and combed hair, the smell of mothballs rising from their side of the church like dew on the Curragh. It doesn't seem so funny now, but at the time it seemed hilarious. My friend was sitting behind me, and every time the priest invited us to stand, or kneel, he'd sing the opening part to 'Rock Your Body'. And then we all started doing it, hiding the noise beneath the shuffle of bodies and the creaking of aeons-old furniture. It will always stand out in my mind as the funniest funeral I've ever been to. We used humour to navigate pain. We all can.

You won't believe me, but some of the best craic I've had has been in silent monasteries. One time I spent a week at a temple in the north of India and I was sharing a bathroom with this old Tibetan monk. I'd been told that this guy was doing a ninety-day silent retreat and not to disturb him, so I made an effort to leave the bathroom if I saw him coming and not to wait outside if he was in there. Our toiletries were on either side of the sink and I noticed that his toothpaste was empty. After five days of seeing that he hadn't replaced it I decided to do something about it. Partly through kindness, but partly because I was on retreat and I was bored, and dying for something useful to do. I'd forgotten that I was supposed to be doing nothing. This is a classic retreat error. I went to the supply room and got him a new tube. I left it in his place with a little flower I'd picked. You become awfully cute when you're stranded in silence for a while.

The next morning he was waiting outside the bathroom with something in his hand. He gave it to me. It was a roll of floss. I smiled at him. The great Tibetan monk was acknowledging my abundant kindness by giving me a gift. He was recognising my radiance, or so I thought. I bowed my head, and then he opened his mouth wide open. He didn't have a tooth in his head. You see, there are some good laughs in meditation, but by and large it's a whole lot of nothing.

Recognising your mistakes and uncovering your blind spots is humbling. Understanding that they will always be there, in some shape or another, is how we can introduce humour into our practice. As Ryōkan's poem goes:

> Last year: foolish monk
> This year: no change

Exercise: Don't take yourself too seriously

When we take ourselves too seriously we stop doing what we want, we stop learning and we stop having fun. The fear of ridicule is very real, but it's also very overblown. Most of us are too busy being self-conscious to be aware of what others are up to.

One of the kindest things you can do for yourself is to drop the standards you set for yourself. Allow yourself to slack off. Drop the ball. Don't always show up on time. Forget something.

Far too often we make ourselves responsible for each and every person around us, and this is exhausting.

Far too often we lose perspective of what's actually happening. It can be important, whenever we're feeling tight or too serious, to ask: What's the worst thing that can happen?

Often we'll notice that the reason we're acting so seriously is because we're afraid of something. But as Seth Godin said, we should learn to dance with fear. As you dance, you realise that 'fear is, in fact, a compass – it's giving me a hint that I might be onto something'.

Relax to Fuck

My purpose was not to persuade anyone to use contraception, just to make clear that it was in no way immoral or sinful. I remember one woman who exclaimed, 'Then what will I have to say in confession?'

— MÁIRE MULLARNEY

I am not against sex and I am not for love. You still have to transcend it. Meditate on it; transcend it. By meditation I mean you have to pass through it fully alert, aware. You must not pass through it blindly, unconsciously. Great bliss is there, but you can pass by blindly and miss it. This blindness has to be transformed; you must become open-eyed. With open eyes, sex can take you on the path of oneness.

— OSHO

We don't talk a huge amount about sex in the meditation community, but we're still thinking about it all the
same. Maybe it's because the vast majority of meditation
literature has been written by virgins, but maybe it's also
just the fact that we humans in general don't talk about
sex that much. Meditators are humans too. They get shy.
They're awkward. You should see a Buddhist disco. I'm
kidding; a Buddhist disco would probably be fun, but it
would almost certainly end quite early.

Buddha himself said that if there was a force on the
planet stronger than sexuality nobody would ever get
enlightened. Buddha wasn't anti-sex. He had a wife and
a child himself before he climbed out of the window in

the middle of the night and gave it all up in the search for the end of human suffering. This is the famous story of the Buddha. It's a hard one to hear, because you know that he left his family behind in order to pursue his life's work. His son and wife eventually became monks too, so in the end, or so we're told, there were no hard feelings. No hard feelings, that's the essence of Buddhism.

But Buddha understood what a strong force sexual energy is. He knew how sex can derail a person. Working with sexual energy is one of the hardest things you can do while meditating. In the temples where young monks were bouncing off the walls with hormones, the teachers would tell them to imagine the objects of their desire as dead or dying. Picture their hair turning grey, their skin becoming thin and translucent and their bones atrophying beneath it. Imagine the smell of their decomposing bodies, the maggots crawling out of their eyeballs, their rotten cadavers stinking in the sun, and then see where your desire is. Okay, enough. I'm done.

Sex is not bad. As an Irish person, I don't think we can hear this enough. But if our only goal in sex is to rub bodies for a quarter of an hour, then we're missing a trick – please don't turn away from the page – when we're not doing sex right, we're missing out on its transcendent power.

Sex can transform a person. When you unite with another person, something in you drops away. The ego experiences a little death. All the years of feeling isolated melt away. That is, if you're doing it right. If you're not, the opposite effect comes into play and you end up feeling hollow and alone.

The mind has no pride. I heard that once when leaving a retreat in Morocco. I'd been living at this centre for a month, most of the time in silence. I was talking to another meditator while we were waiting for a car to drop us back to Marrakech. It's funny; when you come out of a silent retreat, your vocal cords have softened so much that it can take a while to really jump back into the full flow of speech again. It's awkward as anything. You realise in those precious few hours as you're transitioning back from silence to noise that talking is laborious, and yet we're at it so much some of us barely even stop to listen.

'What were your main obstacles?', he asked me.

'Desire,' I said. 'I kept thinking about old partners.'

'Really? I just had songs stuck in my head.'

'I'd happily have swapped sexual fantasies for songs,' I said.

'Don't be so hard on yourself,' he said. 'The mind has no pride.'

It's true. In the same way as we can place the responsibility for our stressful, negative thoughts squarely at the feet of the environment around us, we can also blame our sexual thoughts and our sexual language on how we've been socialised around sex.

I got my sex education from Sister Dominica when I was around fifteen. In my school, we all did. There was no rolling condoms over bananas or squirting lube across our fingers, because neither of those things was mentioned. Sex, according to my school, was a murky, shadowy act and they had no intention to turn the lights on. Instead, we were all brought into the assembly room and shown a video montage of short skirts, flashing lights, young people dancing out of focus and a voiceover that made no sense and just repeated the refrain, 'Be careful and wait,' over and over again. It might have been a Glory Be to the Father at the end of mass. It did nothing to illuminate us, and considering that our sex education was a lo-fi homage to a David Lynch dream sequence, perhaps it was no surprise that so many girls got pregnant as teenagers in my school.

I don't blame the school. It was unfair to ask a nun to try and impart sexual wisdom to us. At home it was the same. I got sexualised, for the most part, by the *Sunday*

World. Dad bought it. It followed him round the house at the weekend. He dragged it from the bathroom to the sitting room, to the table, to the pub, and then home again, where it eventually ended up as bedding for the dog's basket. It was everywhere but I wasn't allowed to look at it because there were topless women on the third page. If my parents caught me, I'd say I was reading the cartoons. They were at the back on page eighty-something. Sometimes I'd even crawl in beside the dog and find them, crumpled, damp, mottled with dog hair, but boobs none the less, in full colour, in my hands. I think I was four.

I grew up with strange ideas about sex. It was very taboo. My very first sexual experiences were drunk and in the dark. We wanted to have sex, but we didn't want to be there at the same time. It was as if we were trying to hide from our own sexuality. Hiding from your sexuality is fine. That is, until you finally sit down to meditate. Meditation is the ultimate unmasking. With nowhere to go, nothing to do, and nothing to attain, we're finally learning to just be with ourselves. All of ourselves. And this is when we sometimes realise that we have sex on the brain.

Never once did someone tell me that sex could be transformative, or even spiritual. This is largely because I barely knew what I was doing. Nuns and tabloids and football changing rooms will only teach you so much. For the rest, you've got to just get lucky.

There are many side-effects to learning to meditate. I never thought I'd forgive my dad, or that I'd learn to listen more than talk, or that I'd finally get over my fear of sharing my feelings. To be honest, I invested in meditation because it felt like a cheaper option to a life spent on Prozac. I wanted a DIY beta-blocker for my panic attacks, and a pick-me-up for my depressive slumps, all in one. I had no idea that I'd end up teaching about it, let alone writing about it from a place of experience. I got lucky when I started to meditate because not only did I learn to understand my mind, I also learned about good sex.

You see, the problem with sex is the same problem with meditation: we think it's about getting somewhere, reaching a certain point. Sure, it can be, but there is also another way. Conscious sex, like meditation, is about being with the present moment with no expectation, no judgement, just acceptance and awareness, and in this way sex can really become a kind of spiritual act.

I'm sorry. I really hadn't expected to write this chapter. This is what happens when you're working late into the night with an unrealistic deadline. Or perhaps it's just what happens during a lockdown when you haven't touched another human for months. If it makes any difference, I'm just as embarrassed as you are. Don't worry, I'll try to make this as quick as possible.

Sex is actually a wonderful opportunity for us to watch our minds in action. Just as sex can get in the way of quietening the mind, the mind can get in the way of us actually enjoying sex. Sex is something that happens to our entire body, yet many of us rarely get out of our head. I've had sex where I was lying there imagining responding to emails and sex where I was thinking about another person. If you can identify with this, it's not an incrimination. I'm really not saying these things are good or bad; but isn't it curious how for long periods of our lives we yearn and pine for the connection that we think we'll get through sex, only to get there and find ourselves wondering whether to upgrade our phone, or if we should have finished that message with a smiley emoji rather than a laughing emoji?

We can bring mindfulness to sex by just being present with the other person and with ourselves. It means undoing so many years of learning to be performative in bed, or learning to have expectations: you do this, then I'll do this, then I'll get you off, then you'll get me off, etc., etc. This isn't connection, this is habitual action, and this is why, for some of us, sex often leaves us feeling drained, confused and empty. When sex isn't conscious, it can actually make you feel more distant from the person rather than closer. I used to think it was just Catholic guilt, and perhaps it is. I'll confess, it took me years to not feel some form of shame about masturbating. It wasn't until I was deep into my twenties that I shook the belief that He was actually watching.

So yes, maybe this book is by your bedside. Perhaps you're reading it before you meet your date, who's running late but texted, so it's not a red flag yet. Maybe you've even just had sex, and while the person who joined in is sleeping like a baby, you're reading these pages. Perhaps you've even given up on sex, which is also fine. Mindfulness, this simple act of paying attention to the present moment without judgement, is something you can most definitely introduce to your love life.

If you've read this far and haven't given up on me, then let me just end with this: As meditators, we don't suppress sex. That's been the message passed down from the pulpit for far too long. When we do suppress it, the natural reaction is that sexual obsessions come to the surface. The mind has no pride, especially the suppressed mind. Mindful sex is our means of transcending so many of our habits, so much of our trauma and so much of our conditioning. Relax to fuck. I love that expression. It works figuratively and literally. Just calm down. Lighten up. It's a reminder to stop clinging to outcomes and just be.

Exercise

An exercise on sex? Sorry, I'm already mortified at having written this chapter.

You know what to do.

Kindness

We have no more right to consume happiness without producing it than to consume wealth without producing it.

— GEORGE BERNARD SHAW

Be kind, for everyone you meet is fighting a hard battle.

— ANON

I can tell immediately when I'm stressed because I'm either eating or cooking or buying more food. If we don't face up to and acknowledge our stress, our body will seek other coping mechanisms. It's like trying to deflate a lilo when you haven't undone the nozzle fully. You're just moving the air around to different parts, but it's not leaving. The same rule applies for all our dysfunctions. If we don't look directly at them, if we don't stick our heads into the lion's mouth, they'll just emerge in unconscious, unhealthy behaviour. We overeat, we text the wrong exes, we increase our amount of time on social media, or binge watch TV shows. Some of us are lucky. Some of us, when we're stressed, just sleep more. God, I wish that was me.

I teach a lot online these days. It's not so bad, actually. I don't mind showing my people my living area as I'm a neat freak, and this just gives me another excuse to tidy. The books on my shelf are colour co-ordinated. I am constantly paring down, throwing away, minimalising. I can't walk past a glass – even in bars and cafés – without picking it up and bringing it to the sink. I don't know where this comes from. My parents' home is like *Storage Wars*. Nurture all they might, they could not divert me from my fastidiously tidy nature.

But this is the thing. I've been teaching people online, as individuals or as teams, twenty tiny squares all staring back at me from bedrooms, sheds and kitchens in Dublin, New York and Berlin. The one thing people have in common is a feeling, whose origin they can't pinpoint, that they need to be productive, they need to get more done. My students would tell me that they just couldn't stop working. That some days, they'd log in at eight in the morning and wouldn't finish until nearly midnight. Yes, there was work to be done – but they couldn't stop doing it. And for those who'd lost their jobs the pressure was even more intense. It wasn't enough to survive the natural catastrophe, they needed to use the occasion to level up, learn a new language, rebrand their business, work on their abs. They were writing impossible to-do lists. Here's a tip: if you want to know how much you actually like yourself, take a look at the to-do lists you write and ask yourself if they're achievable or if they're designed to fail.

I like to get a lot of feedback when I teach. I want to hear other voices in the room. One person spoke up when we were sharing our experiences at the end of the class.

'You know something?' she said. 'We're not adjusting to working at home, we're adjusting to working at home against the backdrop of the most frightening and unpredictable period any of us have ever experienced. This pressure is ridiculous.'

The lesson to learn is to treat yourself with more kindness. Kindness is the secret sauce on the dish called life. Cultivating it is what makes this journey bearable. When we recognise that the world is a dumpster fire, we can fall into despair, and sometimes we need to, but we can also be reminded of this enduring quality that we all have inside us, this hard-to-pin-down but easily recognisable human spirit.

We recognise it at micro levels in our day. We bounce from setback to disappointment to upset to triggering like a pinball. There's no happy ever after on planet Earth. You don't get it right and then it stays right for ever. There is no enlightened retirement. When we commit to exploring our own heart – and, my friends, this is what we mean by exploring the mind – we uncover that, deep down, we're carrying a lot of sadness. Our hearts are really tender. If you could reach in and touch yours you'd see that it doesn't take much to make you cry. It doesn't take a lot to set you off. But we rarely reach in. We build great walls around our hearts to protect ourselves. Meditation is warrior training. We're actually meditating for the good of the world. The more you work on yourself, the nicer you become; but before we can begin to practise kindness on others, we need to start with ourselves.

There's a story about the Dalai Lama. If you ever get the chance to meet him before he dies, I'd recommend it. We shook hands once and I felt electricity run right up to my shoulder. Seriously. This is the story: the Dalai Lama is giving a talk when a member of the audience asks him what to do about self-hatred. The Dalai Lama is confused, so he asks the person to repeat the question. They do. He's still confused, so he turns to his translator for assistance. The translator and the Dalai Lama go back and forth for a few minutes and finally the Dalai Lama turns to the member of the audience and says, 'I thought I had a very good acquaintance with the mind, but now I feel quite ignorant.' Self-hatred wasn't something that he'd come across before. It wasn't something he'd grown up with or experienced, but I imagine that if you're reading this book, you almost certainly have. This is why we need kindness. It's the antidote to self-hatred.

But how do we go about the important work of being kind to ourselves when we've never really been that way to start with?

There's a phenomenon in Ireland, which I'm sure is played out across the globe, but I know it best from my own home, and from all the other homes where I was given ham sandwiches and pint glasses of MiWadi as a kid. Irish women carry out a disproportionate amount of the labour. They always have. There are misogynistic factors at play here. If you're too young to remember, it wasn't so long ago that a woman had to leave her public sector job if she got married in Ireland. Until the Eighth Amendment was repealed, an Irish woman's life was considered equal to that of an unborn child. Three hundred women fought in the War of Independence, but women are still massively underrepresented in Irish politics. Where are their statues and the streets named after them?

The same can be said of meditation. The majority of the books written about it are by male baby boomers.

Most of them are white, too. I've endeavoured as much as possible to include female and diverse voices in the quotations and examples I use, but it's not always easy to remember. This in itself is a mindful act. I've grown up in the same patriarchal soup. Privilege doesn't magically disappear once you've recognised it. Like judgement, self-criticism and doubt, it's something that you have to work on every day.

Our habits are really that deep. Our friends know us well – they roll their eyes when we tell them about our latest relationship, or when we announce that we're going to change something, quit our jobs. I do the same whenever my mother tells me she wants to declutter the house. She does, she really does, the intention is there, but the cluttering habit is so strong that she doesn't follow through.

When someone is treated unfairly for a long enough period of time they will begin to treat themselves unfairly. If you haven't been raised in a calm pool of kindness, it's not enough to realise that and then flick the switch on. This is why we need active kindness.

Kindness will not come naturally to us when we listen too much to our thoughts, so we have to jury-rig it, we have to hack ourselves. It's one of our blind spots. We go along in life not truly aware that our ambition, our refusal to rest, our negative voice, our inability to treat ourselves or seek appropriate medical care is in fact a reflection of just how hard it is to be kind to ourselves and how easy it can be to notice that this is what we do. Thich Nhat Hanh said: 'Suffering is not enough.' We don't need to be so rough on ourselves.

When we meditate and our mind wanders, we don't have to think, 'Oh shit, I've done it again, my mind's a mess.' Instead we can open up a little, shrug it off, look at ourselves with real kindness and think, 'Wow, look at the tools I've been given in this life; no wonder I've had so many hard times.' When we look into our hearts, we're actually looking into all hearts. And when we see the tenderness in ourselves, the sensitivity and the bitterness, our reaction is often to feel shame or disgust, or even self-hatred, but instead we could just show kindness.

This is a poem by the teacher Jack Kornfield. It pretty much sums up our lot.

If you can sit quietly after difficult news;
if in financial downturns you remain perfectly calm;
if you can see your neighbours travel to fantastic
    places without a twinge of jealousy;
if you can happily eat whatever is put on your plate;

if you can fall asleep after a day of running around
without a drink or a pill;
if you can always find contentment just where you are;
– you are probably a dog.

Exercise: On kindness

Sometimes we have to force ourselves to be kind to ourselves. We can do this by simply saying to ourselves the things we might like to hear from others. Right now, what is it that would make you feel good and make you feel loved? Would it be so weird to say those things to yourself? To try to become your own best ally? You can do this as a type of ritual. Go on, I won't tell anyone.

Every morning, when you've finished your meditation just say three things to yourself that you'd like to hear. You can write them on a piece of paper so you remember. It can be simple. To get started I'll give you an example of what my three kind sentences are:

You are worthy
You are brave
You are capable of loving and being loved (even if
you're a ginger).

Forgiveness

In any culture, a woman's mistakes are rarely forgiven.

— ROSALEEN McDONAGH

Holding on to anger is like grasping a hot coal with the intent of throwing it at someone else; you are the one who gets burned.

— BUDDHA

One of the hardest tasks we're ever asked to do as a human is forgive the people who have hurt us. Of all the emotional exercises you'll be offered the chance to perform, forgiveness is like the one-armed pull-up of gym moves. It requires both huge strength and incredible lightness.

There are relative truths and ultimate truths in this universe, and they also apply to you. Yes, you might understand that the ultimate truth is that love is the answer; but you know from life, from dating, from family and from commuting that the relative truth is a very different answer. The relative truth is that some people get under our skin, and some people are so bad to us that it can derail our lives and set us on a course of addiction, co-dependency and self-destruction. As individual as advertising might try to make us believe we are, we're a highly interdependent species, especially when it comes to understanding our feelings and who we are in this world.

But back to forgiveness. I get nervous when I teach this in a meditation class because I know there's a great chance that I'll experience resistance from some people in the room. We can carry hate for so long, you see – even long after the person has died. This hate can be our line in the sand – the thing we'll never cross. You can pry it from our cold, dead hands. Indeed, there are plenty of people who've gone to their death carrying hate. Some might even say that hate accelerates the process.

Hate is one of the most toxic emotions. Feelings of rage and hatred build up in the mind, body and soul, affecting the body's organs and natural processes and grow into even more negativity. This takes its toll on a body in the form of high blood pressure, stress, anxiety, headaches and poor circulation. Think about the last time you felt hatred. If you're sensitive to it, if you can stay with the body, you'll notice that hatred doesn't feel good.

I bought a book just to be told that hatred doesn't feel good?

Yes, I know this is obvious, but really feel it. It's as though you've ingested a poison or there's some spirit inside you. Your body tenses up, your hands sweat, your skull tightens and you can feel a heaviness in your chest as though a weight has been placed on top of you. This is your body on hatred. We have a tendency to bypass the body and return to the intellect. The intellect is safer because it's more supportive of our beliefs and biases, but the body is the truth.

We learn forgiveness as a way of taking care of ourselves. Forgiveness happens when you begin to accept the possibility of change. If you're prepared to accept that change is the one inherent characteristic common to everything in the human experience, then perhaps it applies to hate too, and by extension forgiveness. There's a lot of acceptance in this. Acceptance is the great light bulb moment on the path to awakening. It means we've finally seen the truth. We've pulled back the curtain to see that there's no bogeyman waiting to get us; it's just that someone left the window open. If ignorance is the water we're swimming in, and you've noticed it even in yourself, then why hate someone who still hasn't seen it in themselves yet? That's logical, right? But so hard to do.

About two years ago my dad was admitted to hospital for what felt like the twentieth time in my life. He won't like me for saying this, but there are laboratory mice in research facilities who've had cancer less often than him. When he became ill, I came home indefinitely. This was completely unexpected for me, but be careful what you get into when you start mixing a little Buddhism into your diet. It will start to change you in some very unexpected ways. My dad was in an intensive care unit for nearly three weeks, and in hospital for the best part of two months. He actually had slight withdrawal symptoms when they let him go home. We humans can get used to anything, which is in itself a warning but also perhaps a small mercy.

Deciding to come home and be at my dad's bedside in intensive care, for as long as it took, was a big exercise in forgiveness for me, and I think many of us are tasked with attempting the same exercise. Forgiving parents is probably one of the hardest things you can ever attempt to do. Remembering that they gave you life and fed you is a good way to start.

But there's friction between my generation and our parents' generation. And some delusion too. I go home each Christmas. It doesn't matter where I'm living. I've travelled back from America, Australia and even Morocco, where I had been living in a meditation centre out in the desert, and feeling like I could end my days right there, and still felt the kick to go home. I'm not surprised by this. All my pals come home too. We meet in Dublin, in bars that we used to drink in, and try our best to fit in, in a city that's replaced us.

This feeling of being replaced continues when we go home. We have a unique relationship to family obligation in Ireland. It's a habit that goes unquestioned. I don't have many Irish friends who've cut toxic family members completely out of their life, but it's not rare for me to hear American and German friends say that they haven't seen their mother or father in many, many years.

My father is a very beautiful, loving, romantic man with a heart the size of a semi-d. He's a daily inspiration. Ten years ago I could never have imagined writing that sentence.

If you've never been in an intensive care unit, you're not missing out. They are ghastly, twenty-four-hour halls of light and cables and folks too ill to do anything other than poop in their beds. People die in ICU and if you're a fellow patient you get to see them pass. You don't miss a thing. You couldn't. The rooms are windowless and lit up like a torch aggressively pointed at your face. In the middle of this was my dad, in one of those paper gowns, dry lips, bug eyes and enough morphine in him to convert an atheist.

It was frightening just to be in the room with him, yet he lived there for the best part of the month. They loved him in there. As they removed body parts he still managed to flirt with the nurses. As they fed him intravenously, he still engaged in banter with the doctors, and when I came home, rather than fall to pieces and tell me how miserable he was, he was nothing but good craic. If my dad has taught me anything it's how to look on the bright side of life. He could get a laugh on death row.

My dad survived this bout in hospital. They took so many different parts out of him that he's less my dad now than he's ever been, but it's still more or less him. I'll never forget those days in hospital. I actually loved it. We reconnected. I held his hand, while they gave him constant blood transfusions and all the heat passed out of his body. We laughed when he pooped himself or farted, because at that stage he was so disembodied that he couldn't feel anything below the waist.

I'd love to convey in words how wonderful it feels to love a man who it hurt to love for most of my life. I no longer go home with a sense of dread in my belly, or have that feeling of tension when I pick up the phone. I no longer feel triggered. When I think of my dad, I do it with a sense of peace.

There's an interesting behavioural experiment where they ask one group of people to put their hands into freezing water for a few minutes and the water is warmed up towards the end. The other test group just get freezing water. The second group all report that it's terrible, while the first group who experienced the freezing water for the same amount of time, but also experienced a half minute of less freezing water describe it as bad, but not so awful. That's my relationship with my dad. We managed to thaw a lot. If you can do that, all the years of freezing don't seem so bad.

There's an ancient Zen parable called the Second Arrow. I like to retell it as the second bird shit. A man is out walking through the city with his pals, when out of nowhere a bird shits on his shoulder. The shit lands on his shirt and his mates laugh, and he gets so upset by this that long after he's cleaned the shit away with a piece of toilet paper, he's still thinking about it. Only now it's morphed. It's not just 'Why did the bird take a dump on me?', it's 'Why is everything wrong in my life?', 'Why don't I have a bigger car?', 'Why didn't my parents buy me those trainers?', 'Why don't I have a girlfriend who looks like that?', and so on, and so on. If you think like this then you might as well employ a whole team of birds to follow you around the city, shitting on you whenever you step outdoors.

Forgiveness is recognising that bad things happen and seeing that we have a choice to let them go, or hold on to them for the rest of our lives.

Exercise: Loving Kindness meditation

Regardless of how you feel about it, this type of meditation is called Loving Kindness. It might seem kinda soft and touchy-feely, but believe you me, it's one of the most powerful practices you can do. Loving Kindness meditation equips you with the power to love all people. And this is important because if you can't learn to love all people, then hell really is other people.

Loving Kindness meditation is focused on cultivating love and compassion for oneself and then extending those feelings to others. It's sharing the wealth, basically. When you spend five, ten, fifteen, twenty minutes meditating you cultivate a certain amount of positive energy, don't you? You notice it right away. You get up, and you're like, okay, the world's five per cent nicer than when I started off this morning.

As Charlotte Brontë observed: 'Happiness quite unshared can scarcely be called happiness; it has no taste.'

So Loving Kindness meditation is all about sharing the happiness.

You start by visualising a person you are very close to and have strong feelings for, such as a spouse, parent, child or good friend. It's best if this person and you have an uncomplicated relationship. Don't start with the guy who won't return your calls, or the sister you're fighting with. Someone you care about with no complications is your safest place to start. It's got to be someone who it's easy to feel gratitude for, a person who can arouse a sensation of love within you that you can build upon.

You visualise this person and then send them wishes:

> May you be free from suffering
> May you find peace
> May you be happy

Write down three people who could do with some loving kindness from you today.

You can repeat it a couple of times if you like, and you can play around with the wording, but the sentiment should be the same: you want the person to be happy, at peace and free from suffering.

You then visualise yourself and send yourself wishes:

> May I be free from suffering
> May I find peace
> May I be happy

Many people find this part the toughest. Many people find it really hard to wish themselves well. Many people find it awkward to be kind to themselves. Well, you're a meditator now, it's all about being kind to yourself.

Play with Loving Kindness. You can even use it when you walk through the streets, sending wishes (silently of course, we don't want you to get locked up) to passers-by. And you can extend it beyond just us silly humans. You can send wishes of peace, calm and wellbeing toward other living things too, such as plants, animals, trees and the Earth itself. When you get good at it, you can even direct it towards the people in your life who have hurt you and have done you wrong.

As you meditate and begin to understand your own mind, you're also understanding all minds. In the same way that you can see that you're at your worst when you're lost in thoughts, you understand that that's the case with everyone. People are inherently good. But being lost in thoughts all the time makes us act badly.

Purpose

A blind man is no judge of colours.

— IRISH PROVERB

Nothing is absolute. Everything changes,
everything moves, everything revolves,
everything flies and goes away.

— FRIDA KAHLO

My grandmother turned ninety-seven on St Stephen's Day. It's a cursed time of year to have a birthday. Nobody wants to leave the house. Nobody wants to eat another thing. Many people fall ill then, in the same way that marathon runners collapse when they break the finishing tape. Isn't it always wet, but not quite cold enough to feel cosy? If there's a worse day in the year to be born, it's 2 January, but it's not worse by much.

Not long after her birthday, my grandmother tripped, as the elderly tend to do, and ended up with a complicated wrist fracture, which needed an operation. After the operation, she was brought to another hospital for rehabilitation, and while she was there, the world was hit by a pandemic and even though she was now better, she couldn't leave. My grandmother was lucky in life. She had five kids, about twenty grandchildren and god knows how many great-grandchildren who adored her. She lived on her own, kinda rare for a woman that age, but had numerous visitors every day. She had a garden that she took care of or instructed us to take care of. She had a decent quality of life for a human who has nearly reached a full century. And then the pandemic came, and now for the last year, she's been in an institution where the only touch she's received has been from a professional wearing gloves, and the only contact she's had with her family has been a wave from the other side of a window. 'Fuck my life,' she might say.

I don't tell this story to make you sad, but just to make it clear that we never know how things will go. We're never guaranteed a happy ending. Life is unpredictable and uncertain, and the law of nature is such that we know that the good times won't go on for ever. Meditation, in the end, is preparation for the worst days of your life. This doesn't mean that your life is going to become harder, but that tough times are inevitable.

There's a phrase I like to return to over and over again. It was said by the great meditation teacher Shantideva. In the future perhaps the great meditation teachers will have names like Bob and Sarah, but for now you'll have to do with these guys. This is what Shantideva said: 'Even when I do things for others no sense of amazement or conceit arises. It is just like feeding myself. I hope for nothing in return.'

The whole reason we're meditating and doing the work is not actually for ourselves. I know it can appear that it is. You download an app or you start a course or you buy a book like this because something's wrong. You're not sleeping at night, or perhaps you're anxious or maybe you're beginning to notice your heartbeat's getting louder. You're worried, anyway, so you start meditating. And as you meditate something flowers inside you. Alongside the calm and the clarity, a sense of purpose becomes very clear. This sense of purpose is what we refer to in Buddhism as *bodhicitta*. *Bodhi* means 'awake', and *citta* means 'heart and mind'. *Bodhicitta* is a type of longing. I know I've talked about how wanting things is the beginning of your misery, but this is different. This longing is a longing to wake up so that you can better help other people to wake up. It's a desire to be good, not for yourself, but for everyone you meet.

The tragedy of being human is our misdirection. We all live with this sense of suffering, this sense of unsatisfactoriness. This is why we work. It's why we join dating apps.

It's why we open savings accounts, go shopping, drink 'two for one' cocktails on Fridays. We're trying to eliminate the suffering that goes hand in hand with being born a human. Unfortunately, none of these things really works in the long run. Our satisfaction in life actually comes from helping others.

Bodhicitta is a desire to eliminate all neurosis, all confusion, all impurity in yourself so you can be of benefit to others. It's very simple. You want to be good so you can do good. You don't force it, it just grows naturally.

The very first time I went on retreat, I think it was about day six, I went to talk to the teacher because something strange and unsettling was growing in me.

'What is it?' he asked.

'I can't meditate,' I said.

'Why not?'

'I just want to send love to everyone else in the room, I don't want to meditate for myself any more.'

The teacher laughed.

'That's great,' he said, 'but don't worry. Just go back to meditating for yourself, purifying your own mind, you have a long distance yet to go.'

I did. And I still do.

When we talk about waking up, we mean waking up from the belief that our thoughts are real and waking up from the stories we tell ourselves, the need to be right, the attachments we have and so on, but it also means an awakening of the heart. This awakened heart is pretty much the most powerful force we've got on the planet. When your heart is awake, you stop taking things personally. It stops being about you. Instead you begin to instinctively empathise with all those around you.

Okay, quick disclaimer, this doesn't happen after your first meditation session. It may not happen ever. You can consider yourself very fortunate if it does happen though. It's a little bit like you've been chosen for something. Don't we all carry this wish to be chosen? We all have a tiny *bodhicitta* seed inside us.

As I write this I'm thinking about my mother. She's one of those people who other people call a saint. I've grown up with her so I can confirm this. How do you recognise a saint? It's never about them. My mother fields more phone calls and messages in a day than 999. She is wanted. People gravitate towards her. I sometimes don't get a word in. This used to bother me, but now I get it, and I also try to make it less about me. She loves people, and so they naturally come to her. She taught me everything I know about being compassionate.

They say if you want to know how somebody is in their life, look at their death. Take Jesus, for example. Nailed, starved, spat on, betrayed, all his pals in hiding and what does Jesus say? 'Forgive them.' The Bible is not a book I read, and I have no love for the majority of institutions established in the wake of Jesus' death, but those words on the cross, Jesus Christ, don't they give you the shivers?

But my mother. I quiz her often, because as someone who has been through all the therapies, and read all the books, I'm aware that we humans are fragile. If you inspect us closely, all you see are cracks. But that's not my mum. I'm aware that this is a cliché: the Irish boy writing a book eulogising his mother. But, you know, she has enough patience to go round the world twice, and enough love to carry it on her back, and that's deeply impressive.

We sometimes wish our parents were perfect, or that they had tended to us perfectly. This is just because we're scared of the lives we have. Life is perfectly chaotic. There's no one to blame for that.

A warning: don't try too hard to make your family meditate. Wait for them to ask you. I was once an over-zealous young meditator who would have gladly invaded every conversation just to tell people how they were doing life all wrong and that the answer was just to follow the breath. I've learned since to sit on my hands a little longer. So my mother is not much of a meditator – it's not her way

– but the *bodhicitta* seed is as strong in her as in some of the great teachers I've sat with.

Each Christmas when I go home, before catching the flight or taking the bus I'll ask her, 'Is there anything special you want?', and she always replies, 'Just peace'.

This is another cliché, and let's be honest, if there's a subsection of Irish society who have been wrongly socialised to bury their own desires more than Irish mothers, I'd like to see them, but it's not entirely toxic. We all know ordinary people who are warriors of peace, and not just Nelson Mandela, Pema Chödrön or Greta Thunberg. They just go about their business making time for others, helping, taking care of themselves, sure, but caring about themselves, not so much. If you ask them why they do it, the question doesn't make sense to them. They'll often just answer, 'Because it needs to be done.'

It's like everyday heroism. Why did you run into the burning building? I had to. Why did you jump on the attacker? Anyone would have. Why did you donate your kidney to a stranger? It was the right thing to do. This *bodhicitta* nature exists like everyday heroism does, but in a continual, subtle and often non-dramatic way.

This is our purpose.

Our purpose is to awaken this nature in ourselves.

Many of us go through life with a kind of heaviness. I know I did for the first half of my life. I used to think it was Kildare, the bog dragging my mood down, but it was just me. The heavy mood comes from this sense of yearning for connection. You can find flickers of it in friendships, and great bursts of it in love and family, but the connection that will bring an end to the unsatisfactoriness of life is the connection that we develop with ourselves. We spend so much time looking out, when if we actually knew how powerful we are, and how incredible we are, and how perfectly made we are, we'd never need to search outside ourselves again.

Please do this. Give it a try. And when you do you'll notice something so subtle, yet so overwhelming, happens that everything around us becomes soft. We no longer feel the need to pull at things or grasp. We approach each situation with empathy. We become, finally, saintly; or at the very least, we finally let our folks off the hook.

Exercise: Tong Len

Tong Len is a practice for connecting with other people's suffering. The intention is not to make you suffer but actually to open your heart. We come equipped with huge reserves of compassion, and this exercise helps to access them.

It's simple. You imagine someone you know to be suffering. Then you sit down and meditate, and as you're breathing in, you breathe in their suffering, and as you breathe out, you send them love.

It sounds cheesy? Maybe, but try it. You can use this practice whenever you're feeling powerless to help. You can use it while watching the news. You can use it to determine the points of yourself where there is resistance. Often, we find it hard to want to remove other people's suffering.

What Ever Next?

Hi. Thanks for reading so far. We're finally at the end. The problem with meditation is the same problem that there is with sex. No matter how much you describe it to someone, they can't really say they know what you're talking about until they've experienced it for themselves. I probably should have used that analogy back in the chapter about the sex education I got from the Celestine nuns, but it's too late now. It's late, I'm tired, and those pages are already set.

It's like my grandparents from Belfast used to say: 'Some things are better felt than telt.'

So if you've read this far and you find much of this book reasonable, even the parts where I started gushing,

I'd recommend you give this game a try. I recommend you really experience it for yourself. Load up. Fill your boots.

Meditation has changed my life. Earlier today I went for a long walk with a pen and paper and I made a list of how. This is the list.

1. I managed to quit smoking and drinking and eating animals all the time. Sometimes I drink, and sometimes I'll eat my grandmother's shepherd's pie, but I never thought I'd be in a position to control these things, to actually choose.
2. I can walk into a space full of strangers and not feel social anxiety.
3. I actually, honestly, wholeheartedly love my dad. And Mum, if you're reading – you too. Very much.
4. Most of the time I love myself, and if I'm acting self-destructively, I snap out of it pretty soon.
5. I'm happy more than I'm sad.
6. I don't feel so competitive around other men, but yeah, some guys make me puff my chest out like Rambo.
7. I have more time.
8. I'm brave. Even writing this book was an act of bravery that I didn't think I had in me.

9. I still get angry, I still get the blues, I still feel jealous and sorry for myself, but I tend to be able to make sense of it now. The old dreaded confusion has lifted.

10. When the shit is hitting the fan, I understand at a deep level that every single thing will pass.

I had a therapist for a long time in my thirties. I still book a session with him around Christmas so we can chat, and to stay in touch in case I'll need him again. Meditation has been wonderful for me, but so has cognitive therapy, so has drinking more water, so has going to bed a little earlier and limiting my screen time.

My therapist's name is Bojan, and we've never actually met. He lives in Belgrade, and we've spoken on Skype, Facetime, Zoom and the regular old phone, but never in person. I have no idea how tall he is, what his handshake is like, what aftershave he wears. For the entirety of our relationship, Bojan might have been naked from the waist down and I'd never have known. Bojan was there for me at times when I really felt I had no one. He held my hand as I navigated my way through two break-ups and three different countries.

I see no contradiction in seeing a therapist and being a meditator. If anything, meditation will probably open you up to the usefulness of therapy, the usefulness of exercise and the usefulness of taking care of yourself.

Bojan had something he'd say every few sessions when we'd made some kind of breakthrough, or I'd made a decision, or simply when we'd reached the end of a chapter. In hindsight, all we ever seemed to talk about were the decisions I was having a hard time making. That was my mind then. It was a constant battle between options. Do you ever get that way? Indecision paralysis was my default mode. I was like a frozen screen. So solid, so rigid, zero flow. Until I learned otherwise, I thought chests were always meant to be tight.

Bojan didn't tell me what to do. Like a good therapist he never tried to make my mind up for me. But Bojan would say this, and he'd say it often: 'The best is yet to come.' It sounds cheesy, right? Like the kind of thing you might expect from a therapist working in their third language, or an unsolicited TED talk given by your neighbour in their back garden, when you thought you were just coming over for burgers and a spritz.

But the longer I live and the more I grow into this world, the more I believe it's true. If you're on the path, the best is yet to come. It's as inevitable as a burp following a big gulp of fizzy water. If you're reading this, that means you're on the path. To be on the path means to be going in the right direction. The phrase can sound a little over-played. To be honest, a lot of what I write about in this book might seem overplayed and phoney and fake and cheesy. I get this. Someone once told me this: 'If you can't handle the cheesiness, what makes you think you'll handle the freedom?' When you notice yourself becoming a little bit more open to the cheesiness of it all, it's also a good sign that you're now on the path.

Being on the path means very simply that you've begun to recognise that it's all about you and it's all about now, and the money you make, or the person you meet, or the position you achieve in the company won't matter if you can't make peace with yourself now.

It doesn't happen overnight. This is your life's work. Or, if you really dive deep into Buddhist theory, many lives' work. There's no enlightened retirement. Just when you feel you've become comfortable, the next challenge will present itself. Are we living in a simulator? Well, kinda. I mean the testing never stops. There's always another level.

As a meditator, when we see chaos or drama on the horizon, we can smile because it's another chance for learning. 'Thank u, next, I'm so fucking grateful for my ex.' Ariana Grande said that. I bet you never thought you'd read a meditation book with a quote from her in it, but in this age, in this time, when we're all our own teachers, we take the wisdom where we find it.

I bought an old van recently. It breaks down now and then. And each time it does, I'm given the option to play my old stories: you're so unlucky, life is unfair, if only you'd been born with money, why didn't dad teach me mechanics; or to just go, sure look or mushy peas or this too will pass.

And this is the point: you really are your own teacher, and the lessons really are everywhere. I found one bringing out the bins today. I'd been a little pissed off. I was following up on invoices, dealing with a landlord who wouldn't repair a broken window frame and was getting a lot of WhatsApp messages from a group that I could just as easily have put on mute, but I hadn't. I was bringing the bins downstairs and into the yard when I saw a bee moving between the flowers on a windowsill. It was engaged in the very simple activity of collecting nectar, hovering above the flower heads, a couple of seconds on one, then on to the next, and the whole scene struck me with a fierce jealousy. I wanted nothing more than to live with the simplicity of a bee.

I guess that's just 2020 for you. On more than one occasion I've wanted to climb under the covers and yearned for the simplicity of a bee's life. But we don't get to do that. You can't unpeel an orange, and if you're feeling more sensitive, more emotional, then that's just your human spirit being poked.

The world needs warriors for peace right now, but in order to be a warrior we need to heal ourselves. If there's anything I'd love you to take from this book it's this: healing is possible. And we can do it together. I always say that meditation is a team sport. So I'm on your team now, and that means you're also on mine.

Beyond our hurt and beyond our fears there's so much good inside all of us. It will come out if you give it the attention it needs.

Thank you for reading, and in the words of my Serbian therapist who may or may not talk to clients with his trousers on: the best is yet to come.

Frequently Asked Questions

Many people, myself included, feel a bit intimidated when it comes to asking questions – especially regarding meditation. We're dealing with the mind, after all, a deeply personal thing, so if you ask a stupid question what might that say about you? I think it can be useful to remember that we're all a little nuts to begin with. After all, we humans are just making it up as we go along. So with that in mind, there really are no stupid questions when it comes to meditation. Here are some of the questions that I'm asked regularly when I'm teaching.

I could never meditate, could I?

If you have breath in your body, you can meditate. It's not about being good at meditation or having a particular knack for it. It's about finding it challenging and difficult and uncomfortable and doing it anyway, because this is how you learn to love and heal yourself.

Can I meditate with a hangover?

When I first started to meditate I was still a fairly heavy drinker, so yes, I would often meditate with a hangover, and this is what I discovered: it was strangely easier to make yourself meditate. Possibly because when I was hungover my brain was already anaesthetised and less likely to throw to-do lists at me. The fog momentarily switched the inner torturer off. I can remember that it always made the hangover less intense. I used to tell friends about the benefits of meditation, not from a spiritual or transformative sense, but as a pseudo hair-of-the-dog. As I got a little wiser, I stopped drinking as much, and that was the end of meditating with hangovers. So yes, you can, but you may not be doing it for that much longer.

What happens if I fall asleep?

If you fall asleep or feel sleepy while you meditate, don't worry. This is probably just a sign that you're sleep-deprived. When we meditate, we're tuning in to how we really are in this very moment. A lot of the time we don't allow ourselves that opportunity. We push and we struggle against tiredness, but when we meditate the things we've been avoiding get brought to the surface. If you are sleepy or fall asleep when you meditate then perhaps that's what you need. When you wake up, just start again.

My thoughts are too crazy to meditate.

Well, that's kind of part of the whole game to be honest. Meditation is not about controlling your thoughts, it's about not having them control you. So when your thoughts are crazy, and this happens even to long-term meditators, the trick is to just sit there with them, to not run away, to not give up, to just stay present, observing the craziness. By doing this you're learning how to be resilient and how to manage your own craziness.

How am I supposed to sit?

Comfortably, but not too comfortably. Alert, but not too alert. Like you're the happy new owner of a pup and you've let her off the leash in the park. You're keeping a watchful eye on her, but you're also calm and relaxed because what could be more calming and relaxing than watching a pup frolic in grass?

I'm worried that meditation might make me less productive.

This might be true insofar as meditation will inevitably make you kinder to yourself. If you're a workaholic who pushes yourself to the limit, that might change if you meditate. I guess it can be useful to look at the question of productivity. Are you producing a good life for yourself? If your productivity is not in service to you then maybe it'll suffer. But, on the flip side, you will then suffer less.

I don't have the time to do this right now.

That's okay. I completely understand. We're, almost all of us, under ridiculous time pressure. This is society's fault, but we also have to shoulder part of the blame. If you can look at the relationship that you're building with yourself and ask why you won't allow yourself even five minutes to understand, calm and nourish your mind, then maybe that might encourage you to save a little time for meditation.

What's the most important lesson from meditation?

You don't have to create anything. You don't have to become someone. You don't even have to work that hard. All you really need to do is realise what's already in you and bring your attention to that. All the joy and happiness you're waiting for in the future are already inside you right now. You are perfect. Meditation is about recognising your own perfection.

Glossary of Weird Buddhist Terms

Samadhi: a state of intense concentration achieved through meditation. It's when your focus and the thing you are focusing on are one. It's a type of absorption where the mind is no longer lost in thoughts but luminous and mindful. If you ever get there, do write here.

Arahant: this is a term for someone who is very far along the path to enlightenment. In other traditions of Buddhism it means someone who has removed all the unwholesome roots from their life. It's a pretty big deal.

Karma: the sum of a person's actions in this life and in other lives. If you want to look at it more practically it's basically what you do will be done to you. In Buddhism, your karma can determine what happens to you in your next life, and explain what's happened to you in this life. But basically, if you're a human reading this book then it means you've already had pretty great karma.

Duhka: a really important concept in Buddhism, and Hinduism too. It means suffering or dissatisfaction. In Buddhism, it is considered necessary to study and understand the causes and nature of *duhka* in order to overcome it. If you can see where you are bringing more suffering into your life, then you can learn how to stop it.

Sati: the Buddhist word for mindfulness. (Don't confuse it with the Hindu word *sati*, which was the practice of a widow throwing herself on her man's funeral pyre.) *Sati* can also be translated as 'remembering', which is basically what the whole practice is about. We're remembering that we're not our thoughts and we're not our emotions.

Anicca: the belief that all things, including the self, are impermanent and constantly changing. Life is in a constant state of flux.

Moha: this basically means ignorance or delusion. When people act badly, or believe their thoughts or create suffering in their own life, it's because of delusion and ignorance, AKA *moha*.

Acknowledgements

It takes a village to raise a child; I felt like it took an entire planet to get me to meditate and then keep me meditating. I was such a sceptic and such a reluctant meditator. The last guy to get on the dancefloor. So, in no particular order, I'd love to thank the following for pushing and dragging me along: Victoria Larsson, Patrick Blasa, Davide Reale, Pedro Metello, Amy Tuxworth, Sita Young, Renata Har, Te'Devan Kurzweil, Jivasu, Chelsea Netzband, Al Maser, Catherine O'Halloran, Bojan Lapcevic, Ghita Chraibi, Martina McDonald and the lovely English gent I met on my first retreat whose name I never got. I was fed up and close to leaving when he turned to me and said, 'Don't give in. This will change your entire life. Fill your boots.'